Overcome Infidelity

clinicians with tangible,
uide couples through the
ir, there are several key
team, including assess-
ng trust, acknowledging
sues, creating a dynamic
ip, and forgiveness. This
resents a framework for
step. Also included are
t the author has worked
erapist self-care.

rtified sex therapist for
erapist in Ballwin, Mis-
Guide for Clinicians and
co-host of "The About Sex Podcast," at aboutsexpodcast.com, which discusses various sexual health topics weekly. Angela has been interviewed
for magazines, podcasts, radio, and television.

Helping Couples Overcome Infidelity

A Therapist's Manual

Angela Skurtu

Routledge
Taylor & Francis Group

NEW YORK AND LONDON

First published 2018
by Routledge
711 Third Avenue, New York, NY 10017

and by Routledge
2 Park Square, Milton Park, Abingdon, Oxon, OX14 4RN

Routledge is an imprint of the Taylor & Francis Group, an informa business

© 2018 Taylor & Francis

The right of Angela Skurtu to be identified as the author of this work
has been asserted by her in accordance with sections 77 and 78 of the
Copyright, Designs and Patents Act 1988.

Library of Congress Cataloging in Publication Data
A catalog record for this book has been requested

ISBN: 978-1-138-24055-1 (hbk)
ISBN: 978-1-138-24056-8 (pbk)
ISBN: 978-1-315-28329-6 (ebk)

Typeset in Sabon
by Wearset Ltd, Boldon, Tyne and Wear

MIX
Paper from
responsible sources
FSC   FSC™ C013985
www.fsc.org

Printed in the United Kingdom
by Henry Ling Limited

Contents

Preface   vi

Acknowledgments   ix

Milestone 1 Reducing the Impact of the Affair   1

Milestone 2 Acknowledgment of the Pain the Affair Caused   13

Milestone 3 Clarity   27

Milestone 4 Choosing to Stay or Leave   41

Milestone 5 Repairing Unresolved Issues in the Relationship   53

Milestone 6 Rebuilding Trust   62

Milestone 7 Redefining the Relationship   74

Milestone 8 Reclaiming a Healthy Sex Life   83

Milestone 9 Forgiveness   99

References   108
Index   112

Preface

How long does it take for a couple to work through an affair? What are the likely outcomes of an affair? Will the couple stay together or will the couple choose to end their relationship? As a clinician, how should I guide my clients effectively through this problem? Is it possible for married couples to remain monogamous? Should I be encouraging my clients to forgive one another? If so, when?

These questions are a few of the common questions that clinicians are faced with when they try to help their clients work through an affair. If you ask any other therapist who works with couples, the majority of clinicians will report that a high percentage of their practice responsibility involves helping couples work through an affair. While there are books that address affairs from different aspects, there are few manuals that specifically address the important steps therapists need to take to effectively guide clients through this painful process.

This book is attempting to not only answer those questions, but to give honest, down to earth, research based tools, and advice to help your clients. In this book, I will share stories from my clients as well as fellow clinicians; I will discuss interventions that have been helpful, in addition, I will give examples of best and worst-case scenarios so you have an accurate picture of what your clients may need. It is not reasonable to expect that every client in this situation will have a good outcome. I offer both of these scenarios so that you may have some guidance about how to work through things even when a couple is truly struggling. I hope you can learn from some of my mistakes.

The reality is that many of you are working with this problem every day. Some clients come in and are ready to do everything in their power to fix the situation. However, this is only a handful of the clients we see. Many other clients are grappling with the pain infidelity has caused, infatuation with the outside relationship, and debating whether they could ever get over the infidelity.

My name is Angela Skurtu and I am a Missouri licensed marriage and family therapist and AASECT certified sex therapist. Half of my practice revolves around treating couples affected by infidelity. I have been a couples therapist for seven years now. As a sex therapist, I am highly sought after because many of these couples have also struggled with their sex life prior to the occurrence of the infidelity. I am also a speaker; I run a podcast *AboutSexPodcast.com* where we cover various sexual and relationship health tips in depth.

I am also writing this for those of you clinicians who may have been personally affected by an infidelity in some way. Even if you have not been in a relationship that suffered through an infidelity, you may have a friend or family member who has been through it. This topic is likely important to you on a deeper more emotional level as well. Your experiences can affect the way you handle clients in the room. For example, you may find yourself struggling to stay neutral or reacting to the content that you hear from your clients.

As a result, a big goal of this book is to talk to you as both a human and clinician. When we get too clinical, we risk losing our ability to connect with the people we work with at a human level. I encourage you to take this journey with me and truly begin to understand the great challenge that couples go through when they face this issue. As a part of this, I will teach some self-care strategies to help you to care for yourself when you find you are emotionally reacting to these situations.

I am not the first person who has attempted to answer these questions. In addition to this book, you may consider reading any of the following books: Janis Spring's *After the Affair*; Esther Perel's *Mating in Captivity*; Douglas Snyder, Donald Baucom, and Kristina Gordon's *Getting Past the Affair*; John Gottman and Nan Silver's *The 7 Principles for Making Marriage Work*; Michele Weiner Davis's *The Divorce Remedy*; Nancy Gambescia's *Treating Infidelity*; H. Baucom's *Helping Couples Get Past the Affair*. In addition to these texts, I will incorporate recent research related to infidelity throughout my manual.

This book is organized in a very unique way. Through developing my own treatment process, I recognized some very common presenting needs that clients have when working through an affair. As a result, the chapters in this book are titled based on these needs.

I have framed each chapter as a milestone that covers a particular need. Essentially, when clients start to meet each need, it can begin to feel for the client as though they have turned over a new leaf in their treatment process. I use the term milestone to help couples feel a sense of great accomplishment. I do not suggest that these milestones are easily attainable needs or goals. The road to attaining these milestones is often long and challenging, taking months or years for couples to address and fully come to terms with.

"Milestone" also suggests a hopeful outcome, by which couples can attain some sense of sanity among the chaos that ensues after an affair. There is not necessarily a clear way to tell when a client hits a particular milestone, the term is simply a way to describe the progress they are working towards.

I also will refer to clients as "the hurt partner" and "the unfaithful partner." The hurt partner refers to the person who has been affected by their partner's infidelity. The unfaithful partner refers to the person who stepped outside of the relationship (Spring, 2012). For the purposes of this book, an infidelity is defined as *an act emotional or physical that is outside of the agreed upon boundaries of the relationship (spoken or unspoken) and is kept secret from the partner.* We will go into this definition in more detail in Milestone 3.

The chapters cover the basic milestones that couples need to address in order to get through an affair and are ordered as follows: Milestone 1 – Reducing the Impact of the Affair; Milestone 2 – Acknowledgment of the Pain the Affair Caused; Milestone 3 – Clarity; Milestone 4 – Choosing to Stay or Leave; Milestone 5 – Repairing Unresolved Issues in the Relationship; Milestone 6 – Rebuilding Trust; Milestone 7 – Redefining the Relationship; Milestone 8 – Reclaiming a Healthy Sex Life; Milestone 9 – Forgiveness.

While each chapter presents a milestone to work towards, it is important for clinicians to see each milestone as a journey. An affair is a very painful and challenging process to work through. It would be unreasonable to assume that you can cover a milestone in one session. Many of the milestones suggested often take several sessions, several conversations outside of the session, and time to process. I have worked with clients who are still asking the question, "Should I stay or leave?" two years post affair. Don't assume that these milestones are meant to be an easy task.

The milestones are meant to help you organize your work. I am of the opinion that, as clinicians, we should have a reason for every step we take in therapy. Whether it's working within a therapeutic model or following a research based protocol, I have a strategic reason for every step I take. When a client asks why I am doing what I do, I answer with a therapeutic goal I am trying to accomplish. With this book, I would like to help you develop an approach that is grounded in research and best practices. I hope this book can serve as a guide or reference when you find yourself unsure of what step to take next. In general, I like for things to be easy.

I hope this book will give you clear guidance on how to better serve your clients. I hope you can use it as an easy reference to find answers. I also hope the book will provide a respectful debate about the literature and the challenges that both you and your clients will face as result of working through infidelity. Finally, I hope this book can help clinicians tie together some of their resources so that we can provide a higher quality of care to our clients. There are several milestones that couples need to address in order to work through an affair successfully. While an affair is painful, clinicians can help couples to repair the damage it causes, and in some cases improve the couple's relationship satisfaction.

Acknowledgments

I want to thank my husband for all the support and reminders he gave me throughout this process. Writing a book takes a long time. Throughout the process, you asked me how I was doing, praised my efforts, and even offered feedback for how I could improve things. We have grown together through this process and I thank you for it all! I also want to thank my intern, Jaidelynn Rogers. She offered a new set of eyes to my work. Sometimes when you look at the same manuscript over and over again, you miss little mistakes. Thank you for really trying to offer guidance and helpful editing suggestions. Finally, I want to thank Monica Houttuin. She offered coaching and encouragement throughout the process. I go to you when I am tired of all my projects. Thank you for keeping me motivated!

Milestone 1   Reducing the Impact of the Affair

A middle-aged couple enters your therapy room. At first glance, they seem to be holding things together decently. They appear to be exchanging glances toward one another as they sit on your couch. As their therapist, you are not sure quite what the story is going to be, but you can definitely sense this is going to be a unique session. You ask your typical question, "What brings you into therapy today?" With another shared glance, the wife bursts into tears while the husband tries unsuccessfully to both console her and tell you their story. It was an affair. She found his texts with another woman on the phone just a week ago, and their lives have never been the same since.

For clinicians who regularly work with couples, this is not an uncommon story. In fact, for many clinicians this is rapidly becoming the most common case you work with. In my own therapeutic caseload, half of the clients I work with are in different stages of working through an affair. As a clinician you have a big job to help this couple, for many reasons. After an affair, couples experience many painful emotions. Initially, one of the most important tasks you can take is to help your clients avoid making the situation worse. Essentially, this chapter is meant to help you find ways to reduce the impact of the infidelity through crisis stabilization.

This task is incredibly important for several reasons, one being that emotions have a way of making people want to act in the moment. In dialectical behavior therapy (DBT), this is called "action urges" (Linehan, 1993). Each emotion a person experiences comes with a natural action urge. For example, anger has an action urge of wanting to fight or take flight. Sadness has the action urge of withdrawal/isolation or crying. The problem with an affair is that each individual partner in the relationship is likely experiencing multiple emotions at the same time – each one with its own natural action urges.

You will have clients who want to take action; serious actions that may not be the best choice during this high crisis situation. A big part of this chapter is meant to help you guide your clients not to act rashly. Ultimately, your job at the beginning of this type of therapy is to engage clients in crisis management, to validate each of their personal experiences with regards to the affair and the relationship, and to assess for various factors – historical, relational, and personal – that led to the affair and the resulting choices made.

Assessment

When you work with a couple affected by an affair, there are several aspects of the assessment process. First, you need to assess the damage that has been done. Was the affair long-term or short-term? How did the hurt partner find out about what happened? I try to go back and forth, asking each partner to add their part of the story. For example, when Linda and Bill came into session, Linda, the unfaithful partner, started the conversation. She explained that she had been texting other men through Craigslist and having long conversations without Bill knowing.

It is important to let each partner tell their story, but to also give a space for them to have some disagreements initially. It is quite common for the couple to go back and forth a little with their own ideas about the facts. One thing to assess here is how closely their stories align and what information is left to be explored. Some couples like Bill and Linda have already shared the entire story with each other and have already had multiple conversations about what happened and why. When you work with this client, a big part of your job is to start building trust with each partner and normalizing their experience. Building trust is one of the common factors associated with effective therapies (Sprenkle & Blow, 2004).

Other couples are engaged in holding patterns. The unfaithful partner doesn't agree that it could be defined as an affair, while the hurt partner is actively trying to convince their partner of the fact that their action was an affair. In Gottman and Silver's (2015) book, they describe this pattern as a cycle of criticism and defensiveness. The unfaithful partner feels criticized because they are accused of having an affair. They get defensive and turn the confrontation back around to the hurt partner, who becomes more hurt by the fact that their partner will not own up to their mistake. In cases like these, it can be helpful to see each partner in individual sessions to build trust without alienating the other partner. It is important to establish expectations about confidentiality as a couple if you divide clients, especially in the case of infidelity.

If you have a couple who doesn't agree about what is considered an affair, it can be helpful to define an affair for them to rethink the issue. Essentially, an affair is simply a sexual or emotional relationship that took place outside of the partner's awareness and would be considered a breach in the agreed upon relationship boundaries. Put another way, it is a "violation of relationship commitment in which sexual or emotional intimacy, or both is directed away from the primary relationship without consent of one's partner" (Fife et al., 2013, p. 344). Another way of putting it is, "the breaking of trust and the keeping of secrets in an intimate partnership" (Schneider et al., 2012, p. 136).

Part of your assessment process may involve helping the unfaithful partner understand how their actions could be construed as an affair. The challenge is that sometimes the hurt partner has been badgering the unfaithful partner about this point. Even if they do finally agree that the choice they made was an affair, they may be angry about admitting it. As a clinician, you are walking a fine line between validating each partner without alienating the other partner.

Another aspect of assessment is to learn more about the couple as a whole. You should be asking questions about their lives before the affair. What brought them together? How long have they been committed or married? Do they have children? As you ask some of these questions, you may start to find out who knows what about the situation. Some couples want to share the information with the world, while others are so embarrassed that they have told no one.

Role of the Therapist

Helping couples work through an affair is notorious for being incredibly challenging. The reason is that essentially you are managing several roles all at once. Your clients need you to do all of the following: give advice; manage conflict; validate each partner for their individual experience; walk a tightrope between avoiding blame while also ensuring proper responsibility is taken; help them feel sane again; help them commit to therapy. This is a tall order to say the least. Let's look at each role in more detail.

As an advice giver, your job is to try and clarify information for your clients in a way that helps them decide to move forward. It can help if you think of your client's experience as an example of the grief cycle. An affair essentially is a huge loss for both parties. The hurt partner feels a loss for the relationship they once knew and understood. If they have just heard about the affair, you should assume they will be in shock and, potentially, be experiencing some denial, anger, and depression, or any of the components of the grief cycle. What they need at this time from you is guidance on what they should do next and how to manage this grief in a more productive way.

Another role is for you to manage conflict. Since we are discussing the milestone of reducing the impact, your clients need you to pay close attention to the different choices they could make that would cause harm. The longer you work with the problem, the easier it is to identify when something bad is likely to happen. For example, common bad choices people make at this time include: seeking revenge; telling every family member or friend without thinking about the consequences; having a revenge affair; having huge fights that really go nowhere and don't help the situation; talking each other to death or to the point that the unfaithful partner is unapologetic. This list is by no means comprehensive.

When managing conflict, try to find ways to offer choices. Clients tend to respond best when they don't feel forced to make any decision. I will say to clients,

> It may not be a good idea to try to confront the "other" party at this time because things can get violent or ugly. However, I don't know how I would handle myself in this situation. I respect your decision either way, but I am also trying to help you consider the consequences of your actions.

By putting the suggestion this way, I am offering both choices to the client while also respecting the painful grief they are experiencing.

Another role you must play is the supreme validator. We will cover this role in more depth in Chapter 2. Your job as a therapist is to help your clients feel understood and respected. However, you have to walk a very thin line in how you validate a couple addressing an affair. In every couples therapy session, couples need to feel respected and understood by their therapist. However, when you validate one partner, you can easily make the other partner feel alienated. One approach for avoiding this situation is to explain what you are doing to your clients so they know exactly what is going on. Here is an example of what I would say to a client,

> My job is to validate both of you in therapy. If I validate one of you, I can alienate the other person. During sessions, I will point out times when I am doing this so you know that I am not necessarily taking your partner's side and vice versa.

Once this is pointed out, then I can easily explain this at times when a partner starts to get defensive. I remind them validation is not necessarily taking someone's side.

Finally, your job is to help the couple commit to therapy. "Affairs are considered by many experts to be one of the most damaging events for a relationship, second only to physical abuse" (Fife et al., 2013, p. 344). Since an affair is the ultimate betrayal for couples, many couples are left asking the question "Should I stay or should I go?" While we will cover this concept more in Chapter 4, at the beginning of therapy, your job is to take away the need to answer this question, at least for a while. I explain to my couples that in the first three months, most couples are very emotionally reactive. No one makes good decisions when they are highly emotional. Instead of choosing to stay in the relationship, sometimes you can get the couple to solely commit to therapy for the next few months (Fife et al., 2013). This can slowly help the couple to at least start taking steps forward.

This may seem like many roles, but the truth is that affair work is hard for this very reason. It can feel impossible because you need to become comfortable playing multiple roles. Once you are more aware of these roles, it becomes easier to identify which role to use when.

Helpful Interventions

Essentially, this chapter's focus is on how to start the therapeutic process with clients in crisis after an affair. In Dupree et al.'s (2007) article about affair treatment, the authors suggest that the beginning of therapy is broken down into three main parts: de-escalation, assessment, and treatment planning. In the following section, I plan to cover a variety of tools/interventions that you can use as a therapist to perform these three things effectively. However, I encourage you to use these interventions as guides to build upon in your own practice.

Establishing a Timeline

Many couples who come into therapy are struggling with what they should feel. Am I normal? Why is this so hard? I hate him and I love him! I can't stop thinking about this! I establish a rough timeline with couples of what they should expect at each stage of treatment. This timeline tends to help clients feel more comfortable through the process.

The timeline I describe looks like this:

> You should expect the first three months to be the hardest. Most couples report feeling as though they are on an emotional roller coaster with really high highs and very low lows. During the first three months, your job is to try not to make the situation worse, but you will not do this perfectly. Next, during the three to six months after the initial phase, you will have longer periods of calm but still find yourselves going through emotional hurdles randomly. This will throw you off guard, but it is still completely normal. Often when this happens, couples will say things like, "we took three steps back!" You didn't take three steps back, you are just going through the natural emotional ups and downs at a slower rate. Then from nine months and beyond, you will have longer bouts of peace, but will still find yourself getting triggered when certain things come up like special dates or cultural references that remind you of the affair.

One reason this timeline has been very helpful for my clients is that people come into therapy with unrealistic expectations for what it will take to improve the situation. The unfaithful partner usually wants a quick recovery and hates when the situation gets dragged up "again." With this timeline in mind, they are able to reset their plan for what it may take to improve the situation. This timeline also helps the hurt partner feel like they don't have to make a bunch of decisions right away, but they have time to figure out what is best for them.

This timeline comes from watching hundreds of clients work through the affair process. When they know what to expect, they feel less crazy. One thing I have observed is that in these first three months, the hurt partner does not trust any actions the unfaithful partner takes. After that three months passes, the hurt partner tends to become more receptive to relationship changes. I think this happens because after three months, they start to trust that their partner is not going to terminate the relationship.

Avoid Making Big Decisions

When people are emotionally reactive, they tend to make poor decisions. For example, I had a couple named Jim and Jane who were relatively logical people. They were in their early thirties, highly educated and had great senses of humor. However, when they got into a fight, it was as if they were completely different people. They would get very emotionally reactive and go on the defense. They would say mean things like, "I want a divorce," or "You're a terrible person!" When you would ask them if they really thought these things about their partner, they would often have a different story. They would report that this was happening out of anger, but that really they loved their partner very much and never wanted a divorce.

The difficult part about a couple going through an affair is that they have quite a few things to emotionally react to. For this reason, they are at a higher risk for making poor choices. One way to help a couple is to warn them of all the potential poor choices that people tend to make after an affair so they can avoid these choices. The following section will cover a few examples.

One thing couples do to make the situation worse is revenge affairs. For example, I had a couple named Charla and Timothy who had only been married for a year. Timothy had an affair about three months after they got married and Charla found out when Gina called to confess the mistake she had made. Charla then decided to go out for a night on the town without her wedding ring on and see if she could find a guy to have sex with her. She succeeded and then told Timothy what she had done. This started a new wave of arguments about who was right or wrong. She felt justified in that she did not cheat first. He felt deeply hurt because as he said, "Two wrongs do not make a right!"

While I understand the reason people want to take this sort of revenge, it usually only makes the situation worse. As a clinician, you can explain that while it is common for people to commit revenge affairs, if they want to work on things, they should refrain from taking this type of action.

Another bad decision people sometimes make is to commit violence of any kind against their partner or the "other" woman or man. Again, while it is understandable that an affair can produce serious feelings of hurt, anger, and jealousy, violence solves nothing and again makes the situation worse. As a clinician, you can suggest to your clients that if they want to commit an act of violence, they may need a safety plan to keep themselves from following through with the act, specifically because they can be imprisoned for the offense.

A third bad decision people sometimes make is to cleanse themselves of any physical reminders of the affair. For example, James found out that John had fallen in love with Chris and had been sexting with Chris for over six months in their bedroom while James was out of town for work trips. As a result, James wanted to remove everything in the house that reminded him of John's affair. He wanted to burn the bed. He wanted to remove any clothes or underwear John might have worn during the affair. At one point, he even considered uprooting and moving out of their apartment.

While all of these wants are understandable, actually following through with these activities could prove quite costly. After the dust settles, sometimes people regret having made big decisions to move or give up a car. As a clinician, it can be helpful to explain that they should avoid making any big decisions like this until a few months have passed and they aren't as emotionally reactive. Then, if they still want to purge when their reactivity is more controlled, they can make the choice at that time.

A final bad choice that is common is for the hurt partner to essentially "shit" on their partner constantly about the situation. To put it bluntly, they feel they have a right to constantly criticize, blame, and mistreat their partner. The hard thing is that they feel justified in this decision. Long-term, if this behavior keeps up, the unfaithful partner will stop trying to be nice and will start reacting to the rude behavior. Then, the couple essentially gets into a criticism/defensive pattern that is very hard to break.

As a clinician, you may suggest that the hurt partner go to some individual counseling in addition, in order to work through their resentments and bitterness in a more productive way. This list by no means covers all the potential bad choices clients could make, but it at least gives you an idea of what to try and cover with your clients.

I would still validate your clients when they bring up these desires. While your job is to try and prevent chaos, if you are too forceful with these warnings, you may risk alienating the people you are trying to help. I use the both/and approach from DBT (Linehan, 1993). This involves both validating the feelings your clients have while also suggesting the most positive choice in the situation.

> I could see why you would want to kill that man. He destroyed your marriage. Anyone would feel the same way. Your family needs you though. While I get the urge, it might be best to refrain from seeing him if you think you will do anything that could cause you harm in the long run.

Shifting the Conversation

Before suggesting couples have regular conversations outside of therapy, you have to help each partner emotionally regulate. Many of the couples you see may or may not come into session with the ability to emotionally regulate themselves. For clients who do not appear to have these skills, suggesting regular talks may start regular fights about the situation. You may need to spend time teaching them different ways to diffuse their own emotions. The most common model I use for emotion regulation is DBT. If you are familiar with this model, you can begin teaching these clients distress tolerance skills, emotion regulation skills, and interpersonal effectiveness skills (Linehan, 1993). If you are not as familiar with these skills, you can suggest your couples read the book, *The High Conflict Couple*, by Alan Fruzzetti. This book has its basis in DBT and is a self-help book that couples can read to begin using emotion regulation skills.

One specific way I try to shift the way couples talk is to teach them the softened startup (Gottman & Silver, 2015) and two levels of validation (Linehan, 1993). The softened startup encourages partners to work on the way they bring up their complaints. They need to be kind and gentle in their approach. Using "I" statements, discussing feelings and hurts helps the listener hear their partner's words. The levels of validation help both partners become better listeners. Their job is not to fight or prove one another wrong. Instead, their job is to try and understand one another.

Once a couple has these new-found skills, you can suggest they have regular talks to check in with each other between sessions. I encourage couples to talk for 30 minutes to an hour, at the most daily or every other day, about the issues they experience as a result of the affair. Once their conversation has become more productive, these conversations help them in two ways. On the one hand, they are given a regular space to address their issues as a team. On the other hand, it contains the conversation. Instead of being called at work or bringing up the affair in the middle of the night, the couple trusts that there will be time to discuss things and they learn to wait to have their conversation until that time. It also gives each person time to emotionally prepare to have the conversation.

One final thing you can do to help a couple prevent making the situation worse is to make sure the affair is completely over or to offer guidance about how to end an affair. I will cover this particular topic in more depth in Chapter 4, Choosing to Stay or Leave. However, I do want to make it very clear that the decision to stay in the affair during treatment will not have a positive result for the couple. In fact, it can create very bad outcomes if the hurt partner thinks the affair has ended, only to find out that the unfaithful partner is still in contact with the other party.

A Good Story

Judy and David came into session after Judy had committed an affair. They had been in a sexless marriage for years. Over the last three months, Judy had met another man who stayed unnamed for the entirety of the therapy sessions per the couple's request. Judy felt very ashamed of the choice she made to cheat and said that many of the times she was with him involved a lot of heavy drinking. David was incredibly hurt by what Judy had done. For many years, he had wanted to be closer to her, but was disappointed to see their relationship grow further apart each year.

During their first few sessions, I spent some time discussing the various ways that couples can make a situation worse after an affair. There was still some reactivity between them that needed to be brought down. In order to help them talk more about the topic in a productive way, I taught them how to be more empathetic by going over the validation skills. On the website DBTSelfhelp.com, they cover the six levels of validation in a very easy format (Dietz, 2012). In Levels 1 and 2, validation is described as focused listening to the other person and attempts at being non-judgmental. Couples who use these skills work on asking open ended questions, keeping a neutral tone, and really showing curiosity about the other person's point of view. In sessions, we practiced different examples of validation outside of the context of the affair to help them try things differently.

After they had developed the skill, I suggested they talk about the situation either every day or every other day for 30 minutes to an hour. I also suggested they develop a specific way to transition out of the conversation so the rest of the night could be positive. They decided they would transition by stating two or three positive things they noticed about their partner that week.

At their next session, they already reported the week had been more positive. They still struggled some when they tried to talk with each other about the affair, but they appreciated that their talk could be limited to the one-hour time period. Judy liked the conversations because she felt there was an actual end and she didn't feel as overwhelmed when they had the conversations. David found that having the regular conversations to look forward to helped him be less reactive at other parts during the day. This allowed us to start working on other issues while still giving them time to ask questions of each other, work through the affair, and feel as though they understood one another.

A Bad Story

I had one couple, Sarah and Spencer, that came in to improve their relationship. Spencer had an affair with Jana from work for a month but then said it was over and he was working on the relationship. However, as the therapeutic process unfolded, it became clear that he was still in the affair but not revealing this to Sarah or me. I could tell he was lying, but if I called him out, he would just deny the situation. I continued the process despite my gut feeling.

For the first few sessions, I offered guidance about how to reduce the crisis. I explained various ways that couples can reduce harm to one another as they are working through the situation. I suggested he be honest about the details of the situation, including what happened, when, where, how, and when things ended.

As we continued, Sarah would state that she didn't feel like she had all the facts. During their conversations at home, she would feel as though Spencer was holding back pieces of information. She also noticed Spencer still would not touch her or try to be intimate. When she confronted him about these issues, Spencer would state that he needed some space. He wasn't ready to get close again because he was still getting over things. Sarah tried to trust him, but she had her own sneaking suspicions.

One day, Sarah could not hold back her concerns any longer and she decided she would do a little digging to find out if she was correct. She looked through Spencer's phone when he went to the bathroom and found a recent text string that included contacts for the last few weeks. Sarah forwarded these texts to her own phone and waited to confront Spencer during the therapy session.

The next time I saw them, Sarah confronted Spencer. She said, "Spencer, I know you are still contacting Jana." Spencer denied it and called her crazy. Initially, I stopped the interaction and asked Sarah why she felt he was still cheating on her. "I just know it and I want to hear it from him! I want to give him a chance to fess up on his own." Spencer continued to deny it, stating she was crazy and she would never get over this. He then angrily stated, "I am not going to stay in a relationship where there is no trust!" At this, I reminded him that trust is something they would have to build – that it was common for the hurt partner to not be trusting for a while until the unfaithful partner takes actions to show they are trustworthy. I also explained that it is common for trust to take a long time to build.

She continued to press him to no avail. At that point, she pulled out her phone and showed him the texts she had found. At this point he deflected, "I knew I couldn't trust you! You are looking through my phone? That's it. I am done with this." At which point he walked out of the session. I spent a little time talking to Sarah to finish the session, but it was clear that confrontation in this way did not work out. Had I been forewarned, I might have suggested she confront him on her own and then they come into session to process things.

In an ideal situation, Spencer would be ready to make positive changes and to end things with the other party. The reality is that an affair is very enticing for those engaged in it. While logically, the unfaithful partner understands the need to end things, emotionally the choice to do so can be very difficult. After the big reveal, this couple ended sessions and I never heard from them after this.

If you are ever faced with a situation like this, one thing you may suggest is for the partner to confront the other partner alone first. An unfaithful client already knows they have done something wrong, despite what you hear verbally from them. In general, most clients do not like it when things get sprung on them in therapy without prior knowledge. They call it "getting thrown under the bus." A good rule of thumb if you are forewarned is to suggest to your client that they talk about it at home first, and then you help them deal with the aftermath in therapy. However, you should still expect it to be a very tough session.

Your Human Self

I have created this section in each chapter to take care of you as the therapist. The reality is that affair work is very difficult. As therapists, we are expected to do a lot for our clients. However, in this book, I want to cover different ways you can take care of yourself when you work in these settings.

You will likely find yourself thrown for a loop often when you work with people overcoming affairs. Some of the things you personally may struggle with include ethical dilemmas, being triggered by the situations at hand (counter-transference), and disappointment with humanity overall. That last part may sound over-dramatic, but at times I have felt disappointed with humanity. There have been clients who I never expected would cheat because they seem like such kind people. I am not saying that only bad people cheat. I am just saying that this work can have a tendency to bring you down at times. I am here to let you know this is normal and you are not alone.

First, affairs can often create ethical dilemmas for you, especially when you work with two people. In cases like that of Sarah and Spencer above, you will find yourself dealing with couples where one partner is just not willing to end the relationship despite your warnings of the effect this will have on the relationship. While I will cover specific strategies for how to help the unfaithful partner make this decision in Chapter 4, right now I just want to cover how angry this may make you feel as the therapist.

Even if you set the stage for the best possible outcomes and warn people of the potential mistakes they can avoid, the reality is that people are going to do what they want to do regardless of your best advice. Sometimes, you just need to divorce yourself of the outcomes in therapy. We have to do our best to provide helpful treatment, but also it can be helpful to have a few colleagues you vent to when you feel like all the good work went to waste.

Another helpful skill I have used with my own husband is to talk candidly about affairs more with him. There have been many times when I worry about the safety of my own relationship, even though we trust each other. I have found it helpful to bring up different concepts about affairs with him to clarify my thoughts, explore what he feels about the matter, and essentially to remind myself that my relationship is separate from the relationships I work with daily in therapy. Whatever your outlet, make sure you are finding ways to do self-care. Affairs are notorious for being very tough cases and it can have an effect on you personally.

Finally, remember that you are doing the best you can with the situations at hand. Affairs have a way of bringing out the worst in people. The fact is that you are offering a beacon of hope among the chaos. Without you, they would not know where to go or what to do. For that, you are doing a great service to your couples.

Milestone 2 Acknowledgment of the Pain the Affair Caused

Brianna and Harry came into therapy several months after Harry cheated on Brianna. It was a difficult case because Harry's infidelity existed in a gray area. He had made a friend on a game called Second Life. He had become very close with another woman and had even gotten to the point where they were getting married in the game. He had kept this information from his wife Brianna. Brianna knew that he played the game, but she knew very little about the details or what he did in the game. This could technically be called an emotional affair.

She noticed over time Harry spent less and less time with her and more time on his game. She had continued to bug him about how much time he spent on the game. He continued to tell her she was being crazy and she needed to get over it. This was just a game and nothing else. At some point, she recognized his relationship with this other woman had become an emotional affair. While they had never met in person, she still felt very betrayed because he kept the relationship secret. The reason it took a while for them to come into therapy is because she thought it would be easy to get over it since nothing happened in person. However, over the next few months, she still struggled to trust him. Their arguments grew incredibly heated because he refused to define it as an affair while she did define the relationship this way. After a huge fight in which he left the house for a night, they decided to come into therapy.

Infidelity is becoming more and more complex as we develop more mediums for people to cheat on their spouses. Cases like Harry and Brianna's put therapists in a difficult position because it is hard to put your finger on what specifically constitutes an infidelity. Some research suggests that men describe their affairs as more sexual than emotional, while women tend to describe their affairs as more emotional than sexual (Atkins et al., 2005). While this is the typical trend, Harry was clearly engaged in an emotional affair in his online game.

Whether it was clear cut cheating or not, it is hard to admit this fault. For the unfaithful partner to admit full responsibility, they have to swallow their pride and really take an empathetic approach with their partner. It puts them at risk for many future fights, and some people struggle to admit they made a mistake. Many clients do not like the idea of taking full ownership for the choice they made when it comes to infidelity.

The challenge with this position is that the hurt partner is paralyzed without it. Clients who have not received this full acknowledgment will spend hours trying to explain to their partner why they are so hurt, often to no avail. The unfaithful partner puts up their defenses and will not back down. This interaction pattern leaves the couple stuck and unable to improve their situation. In his research article on forgiveness based treatment, Diblasio (2000) suggests that the more empathy that is demonstrated, the easier it is for the hurt partner to forgive. I also suggest that teaching each partner to work on their empathy towards the other party can greatly change the couple's conversations about this topic going forward.

One of the first things I do in this situation is to split up the couple into individual sessions. This allows a space for each client to really tell their story. People need to be met where they are at 100 percent by someone before they are willing to make changes. I see these individual sessions as a chance to really empathize with each person's experience – their struggle with the relationship; their pain as a result of the infidelity; their fears about taking ownership; their fears that taking ownership may mean that they don't get to focus on what is important to them, such as a sexless marriage or chronic fighting.

There are different strategies that I will cover in detail later in the chapter, but ultimately the focus of the beginning of therapy really is to help your clients move out of any extreme positions they each are taking in the relationship. For the hurt partner, I will normalize the pain they are experiencing and give them a space to talk about how their lives have changed. They are allowed to get angry with their partner to me and they are allowed to talk about how much they still love that person.

It is common for both parties to have multiple, mixed feelings about this situation. The biggest thing I focus on is their current needs and ability to assert them respectfully to their partner. To the hurt partner, I might say,

> You will need him to stay with you and within the same hour you will need to be alone. You will want to search through every electronic he owns and then you will immediately hate yourself for checking. It will feel like a knife stabbing you every time you find a new piece of information and yet you will not be able to stop yourself from doing it.

Often this description is incredibly helpful to my hurt clients because they feel so crazy. Your job as their therapist is to help them know they are not crazy, but they are in a crazy-making environment. It is okay for them to feel crazy for a while.

I also encourage the hurt client to assert their needs respectfully. I discourage yelling, name calling or berating, regardless of how bad the infidelity turns out to be. I do encourage them to ask for things such as access to phones or emails, spending more or all of their free time together, taking more alone time together as a couple, and taking time alone individually. If the client appears to be relatively rational or even a reserved person, then I will say,

> It's okay for you to ask for different needs within the same hour. Even if what you are asking for sounds crazy to you, it is better to ask than to keep things to yourself. Your partner still has a choice of whether or not they decide to fulfill the need, but it is very important for you to not hold back.

If the client is more extreme, I might guide them in the types of needs that are helpful that other clients have asked for. There are clients who have an additional mental illness and will have more extreme anxiety or even paranoia beyond the usual amount after an infidelity. For these clients, self-care options and describing the common needs can be helpful.

For the unfaithful partner, I also spend time hearing their story. I offer full acknowledgment of their struggle to let go of the other partner. I listen to the problems they saw in the marriage prior to the infidelity. I also listen when they discuss their confusion with themselves. The unfaithful partner commonly struggles to explain why they did what they did. In Urooj et al.'s 2015 study, they found that men tended to feel worse if the infidelity was sexual while women tend to feel worse about the infidelity if it was emotional.

The biggest challenge here for therapists is being as non-judgmental as possible. Many therapists who have been affected by infidelity are ready to pass judgment on the unfaithful partner. This client can sense your judgment and will likely terminate treatment early if they feel that the therapy is one sided. One way I stay neutral comes from my own value system. I essentially see all people as capable of making mistakes, including myself. When I take time to understand the steps that might lead a client into an affair, I find that they are more trusting of my advice and more willing to take my opinion into consideration.

Often the unfaithful client is relieved to finally talk to another person about the affair. The very nature of the infidelity leaves this person feeling very isolated. They are making decisions impulsively and often don't have another person to talk to other than the person they are in the affair with. Some unfaithful clients are thankful to have the lies off their chest, even if it means it will cause potential problems in the relationship.

Once I have this client's trust, the goal becomes helping them to understand the importance of taking ownership of the infidelity and acknowledging the pain they caused their partner. I will commonly coach my clients in the following way,

Your partner needs to know you understand the weight of the decisions you made. If they feel completely acknowledged and receive a deep apology, they become more willing to hear what you need in the relationship. Essentially, you make this situation better quicker if you try to swallow your pride here. If you do not, it takes a lot longer to work through things.

This does not work perfectly for every person. Even when I tell clients this, sometimes they cannot bring themselves to take action. I don't judge them for struggling, but I always put out the best course of action. Ultimately, they deserve to know what will help, but it is their choice to decide to follow the advice.

One important thing to remember about acknowledgment in an infidelity case is that commonly the hurt partner will need several separate conversations in which the unfaithful partner is willing to take ownership for the pain. One conversation alone does not often do the trick. I try to encourage the unfaithful client to use phrases that reassure their partner and restate their continued understanding of the pain. This may sound something like this: "I am so sorry that what I did caused you to feel this way. I wish I could take it all back"; "I know what I did hurt you. Do you need anything from me right now?"; "I am going to do everything I can to prove to you that I love you."

These statements repeated often and sincerely really do go a long way to improve the situation. Sometimes you will get lucky and have a client who is already taking ownership. In these cases, you can begin to focus on the bigger picture items. I would positively reinforce clients who are starting off in this way and remind them that they will need to continue saying these things for months or even years after the infidelity.

When you have an unfaithful partner who struggles to give acknowledgment, there may be bigger issues you have to cover to help them get there. In Chapters 3 and 4 of this book, I cover specific challenges that are often holding clients back. Essentially, each client has unanswered questions they need to address for themselves before they are capable of taking ownership.

The other thing I coach my clients to do is to meet the hurt partner's needs when they can. The most difficult part of this process is teaching your clients to support each other through the pain. Couples who learn to assert their needs and meet each other's needs tend to fare better than those who get lost in the defensive cycle. I tell all my clients,

My ideal end goal is for you two to be able to identify when you need something and to have a partner who is willing to do anything they can to meet those needs. The more you both commit yourselves to this, the easier it becomes to get through this affair.

I want this goal to go both ways. Initially, it is helpful to focus on meeting the needs of the hurt partner. Long-term, both the hurt partner and the unfaithful partner have needs that must be addressed to truly heal.

Finally, I leave room for failure. The reality is that most couples will make mistakes even as they try to support each other. At the end of my clients' first session, I tell my clients, "Just so you know, you are going to fail. It's okay to fail. Just keep trying and do your best to forgive mistakes along the way." When clients know it is okay to fail, it makes it easier for them to try. In the Lally et al. (2009) study, they found that it can take someone anywhere from 18 to 254 days to form a new habit. I repeat this study to clients because it helps them to know that change takes a while.

Interventions

The interventions listed here are meant to help you address acknowledgment in detail. While two of the interventions really focus more on the hurt partner, I offer guidance for how to give both partners a task to complete. The path to healing truly takes willingness from both partners to explore the hurts in the relationship. One challenge here is that not every couple has had a bad relationship prior to an infidelity. In Estroff Marano's (2012) article about infidelity, she explains that many couples had no previous issues to an infidelity and that it is very possible for a couple to be happy prior to the betrayal.

In these cases, it can be difficult to offer acknowledgment to the unfaithful partner, and it can be helpful to explore the complex emotions the unfaithful individual feels after having done something to hurt their partner. It can be very painful to cause harm to a partner that does not deserve it. This client may still at least need some acknowledgment from you without their partner. Either way, my hope is that these interventions can help you to guide your couples in reconnecting after the affair.

Grief Cycle

During this time of crisis, your clients need to feel as though you understand what they are going through. After an affair is disclosed, the couple starts to go into a type of grief cycle that I playfully refer to as the grief cycle in hyper-drive. Both partners experience this as a couple and get very confused by the different aspects of the cycle. Figure 2.1 offers a view of what the grief cycle looks like in depth.

As you can see in the figure, there are many stages to the grief cycle. There is the initial shock and denial, there is bargaining, depression, anger, and acceptance. The hard thing about an affair is that you will see the hurt partner go through this cycle over and over again. The unfaithful partner will also experience some of this grief as a result of losing the other person they had cheated with, or as a result of losing the relationship they once

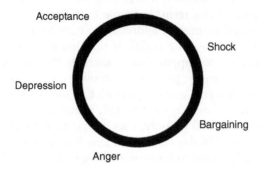

Figure 2.1 Grief Cycle.

had with their partner. The unfaithful partner loses a great deal of trust from the hurt partner. They have to face building a new relationship as a result of their actions.

When a couple first comes in, I show them an image of the grief cycle and explain that their wild feelings are normal and will continue to be difficult for a while. Essentially, I am normalizing their chaos so they don't feel as wrapped up in it. Many of my couples have expressed appreciation for my attempts to describe what they are going through tangibly. This way, they do not feel crazy. I explain that even feeling crazy is a very normal experience after an affair. The biggest challenge they will face is finding a way to grieve productively together and not to take out their emotions on each other. This is the last thing they need at this time. Over the next few sessions, we often talk about each partner's experience with grief. I commonly refer to this experience as a rollercoaster of emotions.

Structured Discussions

In the beginning of treatment, much of your work as a clinician will involve assessing the situation, changing the way your couples talk about the affair, and helping couples start to support each other rather than react negatively towards one another. In their research article about treatment patterns, Dupree et al. (2007) suggest the first stage of treatment should really focus on de-escalation, assessment, and treatment planning. This particular intervention focuses on creating a conversational style the couple can use outside the session to avoid having huge fights.

In your counseling sessions, you will likely use a strategy called "shielded enactments" to help your couples listen to one another respectfully in therapy. This includes "funneling communication through the therapist until the clients are able to speak directly to each other in a constructive manner" (Fife et al., 2013, p. 350). You may need to use shielded enactments for a long period of time at the beginning of treatment. However, it is very important to get your couples talking to each other without your help. While it is great to receive acknowledgment from a therapist, it is much more powerful to experience validation and acknowledgment from a partner.

In this intervention, I have my couples set aside time every day or every other day to have structured discussions about how things are going and how they are working through the infidelity. I suggest they spend 30–60 minutes talking, and I ask them to plan exactly when they will have this conversation. In addition, I ask that they try to limit their talk about infidelity to this time frame. The intervention allows them to compartmentalize the issues to some degree. This way, they know they have a time to talk about the issues. At other times in the day, it allows them to say to themselves, "We will talk about this later today. I am going to focus my attention on work for now."

The worst part of getting through an infidelity for some of my clients is the feeling that the problem bleeds into every area of their lives. The hurt partner hates that they cannot stop thinking about the betrayal, while the unfaithful partner struggles with conversations that feel out of control and go nowhere. One client expressed, "It feels as though we are talking in circles and we get nowhere." When I teach my couples to structure their conversations between sessions, it offers a lot of benefits. It allows the hurt partner to tell themselves, "I will get to talk about this later. So let's just stay focused on what is happening right now." It also encourages the unfaithful partner to stop avoiding the discussion, which exacerbates the issue, and helps ease the unfaithful partner's anxiety about having circular conversations because they know that the conversation has a start and an end. If they do not finish the conversation productively, they understand that they can talk about the issue again another day.

There are a few other things I suggest for these conversations. I will offer a worksheet on how to be validating or supportive during the conversation. I suggest they approach the conversations in the same way they approach therapy – they make a plan for what they want to talk about, they try to listen to each other, and they make the focus problem-solving instead of fighting.

Finally, I give them suggestions for how to end the conversation. At the beginning of treatment, these are tough conversations. It is still going to be hard to have these conversations even though they are structured and time-limited. It helps if couples develop a positive way to end the conversation. Some examples of this could be: to plan for some self-care after the discussion; to end the conversation with things they appreciate about their partner; to end the conversation by watching a funny show or listening to some calming music; to end the conversation with a hug and commitment to keep working at the relationship. Either way, the couple should come up with an ending they both agree to and work on using it.

Finally, I offer a reason for why couples should do this intervention by connecting this activity to trust building. In order to have structured conversations, both partners equally have to do things to build trust with their partner. The unfaithful partner is building trust by committing to a regular discussion, despite how difficult this conversation can be. The hurt partner is building trust by respecting the time limit of the discussion and managing their emotions outside of those time frames. Most of the couples who have committed to using this intervention have stated it was helpful.

Letter of Impact

After finding out about an affair, the hurt partner struggles with a multitude of painful feelings. However, many of the conversations they end up having with their partner tend to be disjointed for a variety of reasons. The unfaithful partner is not always ready to feel remorse. They may even feel justified for their behavior at some points.

The letter of impact is basically a chance for the hurt partner to explore their painful feelings in a format where they get to completely tell their story. The idea for this intervention comes from Spring's (2012) book, *After the Affair*. The hurt partner is asked to write a letter describing the ways that the affair impacted them personally. I usually suggest they take some time to really put their thoughts down on paper. Writing this letter can, in itself, be very therapeutic because it helps the hurt partner sort through all the pain in a non-threatening way. This intervention can be especially helpful in situations where couples are reacting defensively towards one another. The hurt partner gets to put everything they feel down on paper without any interruptions.

The next step is to have the hurt partner read the letter out loud to their partner. As their therapist, you would want to think about the timing of this letter. It is very important for the unfaithful partner to be in a place where they are ready to listen and truly be a friend to the hurt partner. Any reactivity or defensiveness can make the letter feel completely useless to the hurt partner. Before scheduling this session, I explain the importance of having respectful attitudes while the letter is read. I coach the clients to be willing to listen, to avoid interrupting the reading, and to express ownership towards circumstances that caused harm. The letter is not meant to be used as something to hurt each other. It is meant to give the hurt partner a space to grieve. It is also meant to help the unfaithful partner truly understand the impact of the betrayal.

In some cases, I have suggested that both partners write letters to each other. I have seen cases in which the unfaithful partner had felt very abandoned by their partner prior to stepping outside of the marriage. This is actually pretty common in a sexless marriage. The hurt partner will come into therapy with an understanding of why their partner might have cheated – because they had been rejected repeatedly prior to the affair happening. In this situation, it is incredibly important to set some guidelines prior to the reading of the letters. Here is what I typically will suggest.

1   Come with an open mind and willingness to listen to each other.
2   Listen completely to the end of the letter. Don't interrupt, add any-
    thing, or argue with anything that was said. The purpose is to try and
    understand what your partner is feeling.
3   For the writer of the letter, try to end with your hopes for the future of
    the relationship. It is hard to hear the painful information. Knowing
    what you want to see in the relationship going forward can make it
    easier to deal with the pain.
4   If you feel open to it, express remorse for the pain caused and find a
    way to reconnect with some affection.

This fourth step can be deeply connecting for the couple. If you can guide
them to show remorse to one another, it can be a great start to the couple's
healing process.

A Good Story

Michael and Cindy came into session after Michael had cheated on his
wife. Michael had started an affair with a woman, Rhonda, in their friendship circle. He and Rhonda started by running together because they both
were interested in doing a marathon. Initially, Cindy thought nothing of
this because she was also training for a marathon, but had different days
she could train. At the beginning of his relationship with Rhonda, Michael
was very open with Cindy about what they were doing, talking about, and
when they would run together.

There came a point where Cindy started to get uncomfortable with how
close Michael seemed to get with Rhonda. Conversations about her would
come up day-to-day and Cindy would try to point out her concerns.
Michael would tell Cindy she was just being jealous and she needed to get
over herself. After a while, Michael stopped telling her about his relationship with Rhonda, but at that point it had gotten inappropriately close. He
was disengaging from their marriage and even their sex life at times.

Things got worse when the two couples, along with several other couples,
went on a cruise together. Michael and Rhonda seemed to be openly flirting
with each other on the cruise. At times, Michael would make excuses to
leave the family to go spend some "alone" time. Cindy felt this was suspicious and decided to follow him secretly. As she followed him, she saw
Michael walk to Rhonda's room. Cindy saw them go into her room
together. Cindy confronted them both at the room by pounding on the door
and screaming she knew what they were doing. Michael shamefully walked
out of the room while Rhonda stayed back. There was more confrontation,
but Michael convinced Cindy to go back to their own room.

When they got back from the cruise, they made their first therapy
appointment with me. At first, Michael was very angry with how Cindy
handled the situation. The two were not talking well together, so I

separated them into individual sessions. When alone, Cindy cried about how everything she worried was happening was actually true. She knew all along that the relationship was getting too close, and she was very angry about how Michael had handled the situation. I spent as much time as I could validating her hurts and struggles as we sorted through the last few months of their relationship.

When Michael came for his individual appointment, we discussed some of his concerns. He was feeling very disillusioned by the whole situation. On the one hand, he understood he had hurt Cindy deeply, but on the other hand, he was worried that she could never get over things. After the incident on the cruise, he knew he had to make a decision. When he really looked at his relationship, he knew he loved Cindy. He realized he had gotten caught up in the moment with Rhonda and lost his moral compass. He felt horrible for what he had done, but when they talked about the situation, he found himself arguing with Cindy rather than helping or listening to her. This led to a defensive cycle.

The first thing I suggested was that he work on being more validating towards Cindy. I explained to him that his most natural response will be to snap back or to get defensive because talking about the infidelity brings up his shame and guilt for the choices he made. When I pointed this out, he agreed and explained that it was difficult to admit to himself and to Cindy that he had been wrong in his choices. He felt confused because he generally sees himself as a good person and values honesty. It was hard for him to accept that he could also be a liar and make these bad decisions.

I took time to validate his challenge. He struggled admitting that he had made poor decisions, but it was initially easier to talk to me rather than his wife. Once he was able to take ownership alone with me, I encouraged him to try and find ways to take ownership with his wife. Since it would be difficult, I suggested he ask her to just listen and not talk back at first. I asked if he needed to do this in session or if he felt he could do it on his own. He thought it would be more impactful if he did this on his own outside of session. I coached him on how to talk to his wife beforehand and even suggested he might write a letter taking ownership and acknowledging the things he did so he wouldn't forget.

At the next session, the mood between the two of them had changed. Between sessions, Michael had written a letter acknowledging all the ways he had been wrong to his wife Cindy. He took full ownership for the choices he made and he deeply apologized throughout the letter for the various ways he knew he hurt her. He also made a promise to do whatever he could going forward to fix the situation. In session, Cindy reported that while she was still hurt, the letter had helped her to feel as though he cared and he was committed to making things work.

During this session, I explained that many apologies will be needed going forward. Often, individuals can be triggered by day-to-day life events, or even references to infidelity in the media and culture. I encouraged them to try and talk kindly to each other when Cindy feels triggered and for Michael to practice apologizing again when this happens. When couples learn to come to each other for support around this issue, they end up connecting to one another better. I explained that it is common when a person is triggered for the other person to react defensively. The only way to work through this is to practice doing the opposite – being completely supportive and apologetic. This is similar to the skill in DBT called acting the opposite (Linehan, 1993). In the case of working through an infidelity, often the most natural responses of defensiveness have a way of hurting the couple's treatment. It is better to work on changing this behavioral response.

Over time, they got better at this process. Michael wasn't perfect, and sometimes would still react. However, he would apologize afterwards when he remembered. Sometimes, he was able to catch a trigger happening in the moment and respond by offering her support and taking ownership again. It would sound a bit like this, "I am so sorry what I did makes you feel this way. Is there anything you need from me right now?" This allowed Cindy to calm down and sometimes ask for help. She might reply with, "I just need to be alone for a while," or "I could use some cuddle time right now. I need to know you love me." Either way, Cindy could now be supported by Michael rather than start another fight.

A Bad Story

Tiana and Marlon were in therapy to work through his affair. They decided to seek counseling after several fights. Tiana found out that Marlon had cheated long-term with another woman. It started with an emotional connection. They would meet for lunch at work and talk about their struggling marriages. Then it quickly moved to something more. The affair had continued for six months before Tiana was finally sent an anonymous picture of him kissing the other woman in public. At that point, Tiana confronted Marlon. He denied the picture was him and continued to deny that anything had happened. She only was able to fully prove he was having an affair by stealing his phone. It was there she found hundreds of texts and calls to this other woman.

By the time they made it to therapy, most of their conversations had not been productive. He blamed her for not having enough sex with him throughout the years in their relationship. Anytime she would try to get the whole story of what happened during the affair, he would avoid the situation. He would deflect and turn the conversation around or he would avoid having the conversation altogether. In their session, things weren't going so well either. She would scream at him and he would scream back. At this point, I suggested we split up. It was still the first session.

During his individual session, I tried to validate his feelings about the situation. Sometimes clients need to first be acknowledged by their therapists before they can acknowledge the harm they have caused their partner. I spent time exploring his feelings of resentment. Even in the individual session, he was avoiding certain questions. He would change the subject when I asked things like, "What do you think led you to cheat?" or "How do you know that working on your marriage is the best decision?" It seemed that he spent most of the session trying to lead the conversation and actually spent a lot of time still lying. I found his behavior to be somewhat odd.

Every therapist has their own way of setting expectations around confidentiality. In my practice, I set the following expectation:

> Commonly I will split you up into individual sessions. During this time, individuals sometimes bring up secrets they are keeping from their partners. I keep everything that is said in your individual session confidential. However, if you keep a secret that could harm the outcome of therapy or the relationship, I will encourage you to discuss it with your partner. After that, I take a wait and see approach, because I cannot control the choices you make with that information.

I set confidentiality in this way because it allows me to take some liberties in my individual sessions with clients. I have found it can help some clients disclose information to me about the affair that they would not disclose if the session were not confidential. Some therapists prefer to set an expectation that everything said in couples sessions is going to be shared, regardless of whether it was discussed in an individual session. You can decide to follow whatever rule you feel most comfortable using, so long as you are consistent and follow through with the expectations.

I had a sneaking suspicion that he was still in contact with the other woman and had not fully let go of the affair. I knew I had to be assertive but somewhat aloof so I would not lose his commitment to therapy. I explained,

> It is common for people to struggle to let go of the affair partner. You may have fallen in love or just be missing that friendship. I understand why some people struggle with this. However, if you are still talking to this other person, I just need you to know that nothing we do in counseling will work. Your heart will be divided. Instead of fully investing in this relationship, you will find yourself waiting for it to fail and blaming your wife for every failure. When in reality, most change has some successes and some failures naturally. That is a normal part of change. If you are still talking to the other woman, I encourage you to stop.

After this speech, he made a few extra excuses about how he had fully ended it and he would not do that to his wife. I dropped the subject after that point.

In her individual session, I asked her about her struggles. She described that he was very defensive and never really told her any of the details she needed. He seemed to be avoiding the conversation and this was making her angrier and more hurt. I asked her what she would do if he was never able to talk about the situation. She thought about it for a moment. "I guess I hoped it would eventually get easier to talk about. I don't know if I could handle it if we never get to talk. That is why we are here." I explained to her that I would do my best to help him open up. However, there are some clients who refuse to open up no matter what advice is given. I suggested she have a plan for what she will personally do if her partner never can answer her questions or take responsibility for his actions.

We had a few more sessions that went okay. Sometimes they talked decently. Other times I needed to separate them to lower the session's intensity. One day, Tiana sent me an email stating they were not coming back to therapy because Marlon had been in contact with the other woman the entire time. Tiana decided she was separating from Marlon.

While some of our cases will have good endings, the hard part is that there are these difficult cases as well. You can tell your couples what they should do until you are blue in the face. The reality is that some people will still make mistakes or be unwilling to have a conversation acknowledging their partner. In these cases, the best you can do is either help their partner to learn to live with this fact or to make a decision to move on if they cannot live with the relationship. In Tiana's case, it was better to move on than continue in a dishonest relationship.

Your Human Self

Doing this line of work is not for everyone. This is probably the hardest work I have ever done as a therapist. I learned most of these skills in practice with clients. The research currently suggests that half of the couples seeking treatment have either been affected by infidelity in the past or currently (Fife et al., 2013). In my own practice, at least half, if not more, of my clients come to therapy to work through infidelity. As I continue to help clients, I learn more and more ways to help people recover from infidelity. However, it is hard work and it is painful at times.

As a clinician, you are still a human and you will be affected by your work in this subject matter. Over time you will learn all the mistakes that clients tend to make. You will start to know exactly when someone is still lying or cheating on their partner. It will be hard to know that information. While there are various ways you can protect yourself as a clinician, at times it may jade your perspective on committed relationships.

There are many things you can do as a clinician to help yourself. For example, be sure to engage in regular self-care. In addition, I think it can be a good idea to take breaks from infidelity cases. In some circumstances, it may be best to terminate a case and refer it to another therapist. If at any point you are struggling in your own relationship with a potential infidelity, it may be helpful to take time off from counseling altogether if need be. Either way, you are not alone if you do struggle with this type of counseling. We all do to some degree.

Milestone 3 Clarity

Jane and Bob came into therapy after Bob found Jane texting another man in the middle of the night. He noticed she would leave for long periods of time to go to the bathroom. She became very possessive of her phone and would not leave the room without her phone on her person. One night, he stayed up late and took her phone while she slept. Sure enough, he found long text messages shared between her and this other man, Josh. Bob was devastated.

Ever since he found out about the affair, Bob's behavior turned erratic. He began to have unrealistic expectations of her: to keep her phone, to track her every move, and for her to spend all her extra free time with him. Jane understood that he needed to feel safe, but she was feeling very stifled by his need for control.

He also asked her many questions that she had trouble answering. He needed to know how long the affair had gone on for, when it all started, and why she did it. He was heartbroken. When pressed for these answers, Jane genuinely struggled to answer the questions. She had not thought out every choice she had made. Many times, she would answer with, "I don't know," or "I'll have to think about that." This infuriated him even more. To Bob, it did not make sense for her to do something so harmful to the relationship.

Many of your clients will experience this same dilemma. The hurt partner will have millions of questions that mostly pertain to details of the infidelity and the question "Why?" They have had the rug pulled out from under them and often they are in both shock and denial about the situation they are faced with.

Why Do People Cheat?

In order to answer this question, we need to break the answer down into two categories – *rationalizations* and *intentions*. A *rationalization* is how people attempt to justify or explain behaviors with logical reason – even if it is inappropriate. An *intention* is a thing intended – an aim or a plan. When the hurt partner asks questions related to the infidelity, they are often looking for an understanding of both intentions and rationalizations. However, they do not ask for these answers in specific ways. Sometimes when the unfaithful partner tries to answer, they answer in a way that does not satisfy the question.

Consider the following question, "Why did you do this?" If the unfaithful partner answers with an intention such as, "I didn't mean to hurt you. It wasn't about you"; this answer will likely not be satisfying. They will ask again, "That doesn't tell me why you did this? If you didn't want to hurt me, you wouldn't have cheated." The partner might then try to conjure up another potential reason, "I don't know exactly why I did this. I remember being mad at you at times...." At this, a partner will likely jump in with, "I've been mad at you plenty of times, but I never cheated."

You can see how this line of questioning makes it very difficult to explain the behavior. The hurt partner is looking for some understanding of their intention, but the answer is never good enough. Why? There is no noble reason to cheat. Often the answer to why is unsettling. What was your plan in this? How did you cross that line and not think about the effect it would have on me? This creates a very black and white situation for the hurt partner to grapple with. If your intention was to hurt me, then I have a partner who doesn't care about my feelings. If your intention was not to hurt me, then you would not have cheated. Neither answer makes sense given the actions that took place.

Sometimes, it helps to explain to clients the difference between intentions versus rationalizations. Most people don't have very well thought out intentions behind why they cheat. They do, however, have rationalizations they used to make cheating acceptable. Most people have no intention to hurt the people they love. (There are certain personality types that lack empathy for the harm they cause to others. We will discuss these personality types more in Chapter 4.)

Often, the unfaithful partner used various rationalizations as they crossed different boundaries in the relationship. These are things they told themselves so they could live with their actions. When people act outside of their value system, it causes chaos. This is part of the reason why when someone is cheating, a spouse can tell their behavior changes. To some degree, cheating is outside of most people's value system. In order to make certain choices or cross certain boundaries, a person has to find ways to rationalize the situation.

For example, Doug and Ari are co-workers. Each of them is married. Doug and Ari have no intention to do anything to hurt their spouses. They consider themselves good people. One day, Doug wants to go to lunch, but his usual buddy is sick that day. Ari is friendly and outgoing, so he casually invites her to lunch. It is just a friendly work lunch. No big deal. At this point, no poor choices are made and neither person is even considering the possibility that they may cheat on their spouse.

During lunch they talk casually until one of them expresses a piece of information that is a little more vulnerable. Doug offered to pay for lunch, to which Ari replied, "I wish my husband would pay for things once in a while." She initially wasn't planning to share any personal information, but she maybe rationalizes her choice by saying to herself, "It's no big deal. People talk about their spouses all the time. By talking about my husband, at least he knows I am married." At the opening of vulnerable information, Doug suddenly feels safer to talk about his issues. He states, "My wife and I are having problems too. She stays out late most nights to go out with her friends...." He might rationalize this conversation by saying to himself, "We both have relationship issues. There's no harm in making a friend."

Over the course of their affair, they each will use small rationalizations to justify the choices they make. When he first sends a flirty text, he may rationalize it by saying to himself, "My wife isn't home. She clearly doesn't care about me. Besides, it's just harmless flirting. People do it all the time." When she first accepts this flirtation, she may rationalize the behavior by saying to herself, "I know he likes me, but I would never cheat. This is just playful talking. Besides, what my husband doesn't know won't hurt him." As they pass each boundary, they each may develop their own rationalization for the behavior. It's a way of compartmentalizing the affair. The more rationalizations they use, the easier it becomes to take the next steps towards an emotional or physical affair. Essentially the explanation for an infidelity is a complex pairing of rationalizations combined with intense feelings of desire, excitement, and taboo.

The odd part of all of this is that through each choice, most unfaithful partners will explain they still had no intention of hurting their partner. Some will even state they never thought about how their choices would affect their partner. Even when they make decisions that could affect the relationship significantly, by the time they get to this point, they have already found some way to compartmentalize the choice they are making.

You can see how a person has rationalized a situation by what happens next. The unfaithful partner often tries to withhold information after the affair is found out. Even when all the evidence points to the fact that they cheated, they still don't want to share everything with their partner. Even after everything is out, they still do not want to hurt their partner. Once they are facing the terrible choice they made, it becomes hard for them to face themselves, let alone their partner.

You will see the unfaithful partner get very confused after the fact. In many cases, the unfaithful partner never thought about the "whys," they only rationalized the choices. A good visual for this is to think about a variety of squares.

Imagine that a person's heart is at the center of this image. Each square that leads to the next is an example of a boundary that a person uses to guard their heart or protect their marriage.

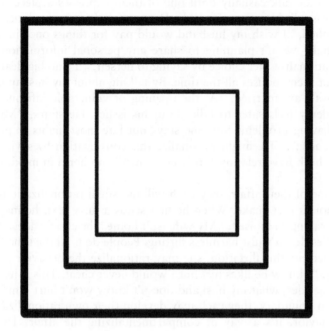

Figure 3.1 Boundaries that Protect the Heart.

Most people don't start an affair with having sex or falling in love. That would be the square or boundary closest to the heart. Most people start somewhere further out. In the example of Doug and Ari above, they first crossed a boundary when she shared her disappointment in her partner. This would represent the furthest out square. When she shared, she let him into the next space. He accepted by offering his own commiseration. Each time a square or boundary is crossed, there is usually a rationalization needed to cross that boundary.

Once one square is crossed, it is odd how easy it becomes to allow someone closer and closer. Until one day, they do have sex or they do fall in love. Depending on when their partner finds out, it can become harder for them to remove the other woman/man from the inner square. As we all know, love is a very powerful emotion.

Understanding the Timeline of Treatment

It takes people roughly around three months to get through the initial crisis. After the final piece of new information is clarified, the timeline starts. If new information comes out later, the timeline seems to start over again. This is why I commonly suggest that the unfaithful partner tells every piece of information up front. The hurt person needs full clarity from their partner in order to begin to trust that their partner is invested in the relationship. Once they get this clarity, they start building trust in their partner's investment.

In the initial months after the infidelity, you commonly see the hurt partner engaging in tracking behavior. It is most important to the hurt partner to see that their partner is physically where they say they are. They need willingness from their partner to allow some tracking behaviors. Unfaithful partners who are unwilling and/or defensive about the tracking behaviors tend to make the situation worse because they are unwilling to do anything to hold themselves accountable to their partner. Once the partner trusts that their partner will not leave, you will see the tracking behaviors die down and more of the focus will be paid to improving the original problems of the relationship. This is also why, even though couples are trying to do as much as possible to make their relationship strong, that trust is not built yet. Couples first must create trust in their willingness to stay together. After reducing the initial crisis, the relationship work begins.

It is important to remember that tracking behaviors can be very annoying and somewhat invasive. As the clinician, you want to observe for any abusive behaviors or overly obtrusive behaviors. While I understand a hurt partner's need to track, this doesn't actually rebuild any sort of trust. In fact, it can have the opposite effect. The hurt partner gets angry that they "have" to track their partner's movements. They do not wish to live in a relationship where this will be necessary long-term. It can be good to reassure each partner that what is more important is the willingness to be tracked rather than the actual tracking. Often when a hurt partner sees the unfaithful partner willingly giving up some freedoms to build trust, this helps the hurt partner let go of some of these tracking behaviors. (In some extreme cases, you may have to point out if the hurt partner appears to be asking for too much.)

Interventions

The following interventions are meant to help each partner find some clarity in the midst of the chaos. Without clarity, I often find that either partner can suffer from a lack of closure. Some continue to struggle for years beyond the infidelity. Even an unfaithful partner can struggle with daunting questions about whether they have made the best decision. In this section, and also in the next chapter, I cover various ways to help your clients find answers to their questions.

Defining the Affair

One of the first goals in treatment may be to help the couple agree to a similar definition about what constitutes an affair. Many couples come into therapy bickering about what is truly considered an infidelity. I think this happens partially because the unfaithful partner struggles with being seen as a bad person or feeling blamed. Sometimes it's easier to deny you did something wrong than admit that you betrayed your partner's trust.

The problem with this mentality is that it makes the situation worse. Instead of starting to support each other through this time in the relationship, the couple finds themselves bickering over semantics. It is helpful to define the term "infidelity" out loud to both partners when this is happening. According to Berman & Frazier (2005), infidelity is defined as "a romantic, sexual, or emotional relationship with someone other than the primary partner that was kept secret from the partner and that would have been unacceptable to the partner if s/he had known" (p. 1620). I break this definition down with my clients even more simply by saying an infidelity is any relationship with someone outside of the relationship that is kept secret from their spouse/partner. The secrecy is enough for most people to feel as though they have been betrayed.

When you as the clinician find a neutral and respectful way to define infidelity to both parties, it makes it easier to stop the bickering between them. Essentially what you are trying to convey is that it doesn't matter exactly how they did what they did, what matters most is to help them work through the betrayal as a team. Ultimately, it matters a great deal to the hurt partner because if they cannot agree on a definition, then they are at risk of being hurt again. This means their partner could flirt with the boundaries of the relationship again and still find an excuse for telling their partner they are over-reacting.

Once you define the infidelity, the goal is to help each person come to terms with this definition and what it means for them individually. For the unfaithful partner, it may mean they have to face their feelings of guilt and admit to their partner they understand that they caused harm. For the hurt partner, they may now struggle with how long it took for their partner to accept their betrayal, or they may be resentful that a clinician had to define it in order for the unfaithful partner to really hear the problem. Throughout any of these reactions, your goal as a therapist should be to show empathy to both clients and try to help them to start supporting each other.

Dancing with the Devil

The unfaithful partner is likely coming into therapy assuming they will be dragged through the coals with you as a therapist. They have committed the ultimate "sin" which is betraying their partner's trust. This very stance can often make it difficult to connect with the unfaithful partner as a therapist – especially if they feel justified in their actions.

This particular intervention should only be done in a solo session with the unfaithful partner as a means to build some rapport with this client. Obviously, this takes some comfort on the level of the therapist. Basically, your job is to suggest that the affair might have been a nice or wonderful experience for this person. Here is an example of how this conversation would go,

> Many people in your position struggle because you are supposed to feel terrible about what you did. While in reality, the affair was a wonderful experience. Many people in your position feel as though the affair rejuvenated them in some way. It makes them feel alive, awakened. While you understand that the choice caused harm to your partner, you also needed something like this for yourself. What are your thoughts?

I call this intervention dancing with the devil because essentially you are playing devil's advocate. You are giving them a safe space to explore the positive feelings they may have as a result of the affair. This can be considered a variation of the both/and approach from DBT (Fruzzetti, 2006). The goal is to be completely non-judgmental and fully meet this client where they are at, rather than judge or condemn them like everyone else has.

As a therapist, you are giving them permission to explore their feelings – all of them – good, bad, and indifferent. This intervention is particularly helpful with clients who are very adamantly opposed to admitting they may be wrong in this situation. How can they feel wrong when everything about the situation felt positive (except for their partner's reaction)?

What I have found is that once a client is met with understanding and willingness, then they are more open to change. The both/and approach suggests that you can be both validating and also suggest pro-social behaviors. From showing a very deep respect and understanding for where this client is at emotionally, then they can be more willing to consider their partner's perspective. Usually, this is the point where I can turn the session around to the other person. Here is an example, "It must be very difficult to have experienced such pleasure from an experience that caused so much pain to those around you. What is this like for you?"

As you can imagine, a client might then respond with more empathy for their partner. One client stated,

> I know I hurt her so badly. It just makes me so angry when she asks me all these questions and expects me to feel how I don't feel. She abandoned me for years! What did she expect would happen?

If you are continuing to use the both/and approach, you might respond with both a validation and push for change,

> I bet there were years you felt abandoned. Maybe you rejected other suitors in the past in order to preserve the marriage, only to be rejected

by the very person you are supposed to be loved and accepted by. Since you know what that abandonment feels like, you probably know exactly how your wife feels now – abandoned and rejected.

As you can see in this example, every word spoken is chosen strategically. You have to show the unfaithful client that you deeply respect and understand how they could have made the decision to step out of their marriage. Even though most people would agree that infidelity is wrong and unthinkable, if this client feels shamed by you, they will lose some trust in you as a clinician. If you take a moment to "dance with the devil," you may gain their trust and willingness to change. I have worked with clients for seven years now, and anytime I meet resistance, I move towards deep validation. Often when you meet a person 100 percent where they are at, then they can trust you to guide them towards change.

To Contact or Not Contact the 'Other' Man/Woman/Person

Rhianna and Dana came into therapy after Dana found Rhianna and Patty's multiple shared text messages. Dana had confronted Rhianna about her affair. Rhianna admitted what she did was wrong and was ready to work on things. While Dana was grateful for her choice to focus on the marriage, she still felt an intense urge to contact Patty to find out more information. She always felt that Rhianna was keeping information from her, despite the various ways she tried to ask to understand the situation. I could tell Rhianna was holding back some as well.

It is quite common for the hurt partner to battle with the thought of whether to contact or not contact the outside party. They want to do this for a variety of reasons. Sometimes, they want to hear all the information before they make the decision to move forward with the healing process. Sometimes, they want to know if this outside person is still a threat and are seeking to put them in their place. Other times, they want to let that other person know how much harm they caused in the relationship. Either way, at some point, the hurt partner will likely need to talk to you about what choice they should make regarding this contact.

My usual suggestion is to identify the goal they have for contacting this person first. Once I understand their goal, then I try to offer to the best of my knowledge some pros and cons for making the choice to contact that person. I also usually suggest they think about this decision for a while before acting on it. When your clients are in an emotional state, they sometimes make rash decisions without any forethought. Asking your clients to wait to contact the other person is your way of giving them a chance to think about the decision in a more logical way. They may still do it, but at least when they do, they will have a plan for what they want to say. Hopefully, this will keep things from dragging out or becoming dramatic.

In Dana's case, she wanted to contact Patty's wife as well to let her know about the relationship Rhianna and Patty shared. She also wanted to put Patty in her place by confronting her. Some part of Dana also wanted revenge. She wanted Patty to hurt in the same way that she was hurting – going through the aftermath of the affair.

In this scenario, I suggested that Dana take some time to write a letter for herself first. In this letter, she could say everything she wanted to say to Patty. I warned her not to send the letter. Instead, it was meant to be a journaling activity in which she had a chance to get out all her hurt feelings in a less destructive way. I also asked that if she did want to send a letter, that she run it by me first so we could make sure there were no incriminating statements in the letter.

Dana spent several weeks journaling about all the things she hated about Patty – all the ways she hurt their relationship. Over the weeks, we continued to discuss the situation in therapy. Dana finally decided she wanted to send a text with Rhianna as a team to Patty, asking her to never contact Rhianna or anyone in their family again. In that text, Dana shared that if Patty did contact Rhianna again, she would share all of the information about the affair with Patty's wife. Patty did not respond to the text or contact Rhianna ever again. Finally, Dana felt some peace.

I never tell people exactly what they should or should not do in these scenarios because I am not sure if there is a perfect answer for how you should handle the situation. If it happened to me, I could easily see a part of me that would want revenge or would want to somehow make that person feel the hurt I was feeling. The reality is that I have also seen couples get lost in a lot of unnecessary drama and even turn to violence in these situations. If anything, therapy should be a place where you help your client explore the options and make the decision that they feel most at peace doing, even if that means not doing anything at all.

Helping the Unfaithful Partner End the Affair

Many unfaithful clients really struggle to end their affairs, even in the face of possibly losing their spouses. Some clinicians struggle with whether or not to encourage a step in this direction or not because the decision can be complex. Does the unfaithful partner work with this person? Is the person in the same friend group? Was this other person initially a good friend that the unfaithful partner still values having in their life? Is it possible to set boundaries around the relationship and not hurt the marriage?

I am going to be honest with you all and state that I am biased on this particular topic. I truly believe if the couple is trying to work on their relationship, the best route is to end all contact with the other person. I have seen so many clients try to put boundaries around these affairs only to fall back into the relationship again over time. Some people would say it is possible to keep the "other" person at a safe distance with good boundaries.

However, I personally err on the side of caution, especially if the clients both are stating they want to save their marriage/long-term relationship.

Here's the problem: even though clients are paying you to tell them what to do, they also have a natural tendency to be willful if they feel they are forced to do anything. People value choice and feeling in control of their personal lives. As clinicians, when we force clients or shame them into making the "right decision," they will naturally crave the opposite because it is now forbidden. What could be more forbidden than an affair?

I take the approach of offering information about what can happen if they continue in the other relationship and what can happen if they end it. I try to offer as much information about the pros and cons I have seen with past clients and I always suggest that the unfaithful client make the best choice for themselves. Naturally, as I am biased, I try to paint a picture in which ending the other relationship appears to be the better choice.

Here is an example:

> It is very common for people in your position to struggle letting go of this old relationship. You feel a lot of connection to this new person and you aren't sure if you want to stay or leave your current relationship. You can try to set boundaries around this relationship, but it will hurt your spouse. There may be too many gray areas to really control the circumstances. On the flip-side, many clients who keep this person in their life do things to undermine the therapy process. They will only do the interventions halfway and every time something goes wrong, they will easily blame their partner. The problem with this is that change naturally has ups and downs. By removing this other person, you can really focus on seeing if this current relationship can be repaired.

This sometimes works and sometimes does not. When clients really love the new person and are struggling with the idea of losing them, it can truly be difficult to end the new relationship. In these situations, you may need to spend several individual sessions exploring their personal struggle. In some scenarios, it can be a good idea to refer a client to individual therapy as well as couples counseling to give them more time to explore the best path.

A Good Story

Sarah and Liona were in therapy because Liona had an affair when they were on a relationship break. Sarah and Liona's relationship started as an affair. Liona was with another woman and their relationship had not been going well for a very long time. Around that time, Sarah started working with Liona. They would flirt and talk on the phone constantly, until one day when Sarah's girlfriend found out and they broke up.

At this point, Sarah and Liona were on and off again for a while with one another for various reasons. Sarah was not sure what she wanted and did try counseling with her previous girlfriend to make it work. During that counseling, she still found herself going back to Liona. At the time, Liona was getting resentful of the back and forth. During one of their breaks, Liona dated someone else for a time and did not tell Sarah. Eventually, Sarah left her partner and more firmly committed to Liona.

They had been together for two years and worked through many issues with each other. Recently, Sarah found out that Liona had dated someone on their break and was very heartbroken. They came into session soon after this happened. Sarah was completely heartbroken and felt as though Liona had cheated. Liona had trouble seeing it this way because they were on a break.

During their first session, I offered a definition of infidelity. Basically, infidelity is when one person keeps a secret from another person about what they are doing with another person. It can be sexual or emotional. If it is kept secret and the people in the relationship had an agreement about how their relationship was defined, then any stepping outside of that agreement is considered an infidelity. After hearing the definition, Liona understood why it might be difficult for Sarah to hear this new information. While they were on a break, they were still in contact and Sarah told her she loved her. At this point, she acknowledged openly with Sarah that she could see why this action hurt her.

The interesting thing is that this helped Sarah to acknowledge how she might have hurt her partner. Liona loved her and wanted to be with her. At the time, Sarah still had unfinished business with her previous partner. Sarah could now see why Liona lashed out and started another relationship. Even though she verbally was trying to stay connected with Liona, her actions showed that she was trying to stay with her former lover. This didn't fix the entire situation, but it did help them start working better together in therapy.

A Bad Story

Marjorie and Dennis had been married for 25 years. Most of their marriage had been uneventful except for the previous five years, in which they had grown apart both emotionally and sexually. It seemed as though Dennis and Marjorie lived separate lives. Marjorie was constantly spending time with her family and her friends, while Dennis had started going out to bars more on his own. They also worked separate schedules – Dennis worked the third shift while Marjorie worked the first shift.

Everything seemed to come to a head when Marjorie found out that Dennis had cheated on her with a woman he met at the bar. She had noticed their distance and that they had been fighting about random little things. She checked his phone and found messages from this other woman

– Jill. Marjorie immediately called Jill to find out more about what they had done and to catch Dennis in the act. Jill answered, but when she saw that it was Dennis's wife, she immediately hung up the phone and avoided answering her phone calls.

Marjorie then confronted Dennis, who denied the affair several times until Marjorie showed him the evidence she found on his phone. Even after Marjorie showed him the messages she had seen, he still wouldn't talk willingly with her about the situation. He would get highly defensive and tell her he didn't want to get into it.

Weeks later, Marjorie and Dennis were in therapy with me, trying to sort through all the hurt feelings. As per my usual, I suggested to the hurt partner that she pick and choose which information she would like to hear. I always explain that there is this incessant need to know everything, but that every time she hears something new, it will kill her (figuratively speaking). I also suggested to the unfaithful partner that he take himself out of the position of picking and choosing what information to give his partner and just try to be honest.

Clarity is one of the most painful needs a couple has when working through an affair, but if the hurt partner – Marjorie – doesn't get the clarity she needs to move on, it can be devastating and difficult to move forward. As the weeks went on, Dennis repeatedly avoided any effort to give Marjorie the facts she needed. In session, when I tried to encourage him to answer different questions, he would get reactive and defensive. He would also often turn the session toward blaming Marjorie for emotionally abandoning him during the relationship. I tried to empathize with him and state things like, "I could see why you felt abandoned. It must have felt like you were no longer married at times." No matter what tactic I used, I could not get him to help her out with the information.

As a clinician, you have likely been in this position. One of the hardest parts of working with a couple affected by an affair is when you see the potential good choice a client could make to fix things, and you see them repeatedly avoid making the good choice. This is a scenario where there were not going to be great outcomes.

It is still our job to try and help people get to a better spot. I decided to meet with this couple individually. For Marjorie, I asked her if she could move forward if she never got the answers. I asked, "What if he can never bring his defenses down enough to tell you what you need to know? Could you still move forward or would this be an end to the relationship?" Marjorie responded with, "Well, I don't know. We are very good to each other if we don't talk about it, but then I am left to deal with it in my own head. I really struggle with that." As I counseled her further, I suggested that maybe we could do a session in which I ask all the questions she needs answered. I explained to her that her husband would have to be on board and that she would probably never get another session like this again. She agreed and told me the questions she wanted me to ask.

In my individual session with Dennis, I discussed how difficult it must be for him to keep hearing her bring up the same questions. He stated, "It's like she can't get over it. I tell her, all you do is start a fight when you bring this up." I explained that he probably had not given her the answers she needed to move on and until she got those answers, she would likely keep asking the same questions. From there, I then brought up the same idea I posed to his wife. "What if I controlled the questions? I kept her from reacting to your answers, but asked the things she needed to help her move forward. Would you be willing to have this session?" The rest of the session involved some negotiating of boundaries on his end, but he reluctantly agreed.

In the couple session, my aim was to address the most important information. As suggested in Fife et al. (2013), I kept my questions to factual information about the identity of the extramarital partner, the duration of the affair, the frequency and the location of the meetings. Luckily these are the only questions that Marjorie wanted answered. The intervention I used was called a shielded enactment, which is where all communication is funneled through me, the therapist, to keep the session constructive (Butler & Gardner, 2003). There were times when Marjorie wanted to jump in, but I would immediately and kindly ask her to let me lead so she could get the information she needed. I would at the same time encourage Dennis to keep answering to the best of his ability, reminding him that what he was doing would allow her to heal.

We got the basic information completed by the end of the session, but it was no easy task. In an ideal situation, this could have been the start of potential healing conversations, but the reality is that not all our sessions will have perfect outcomes. This session was the first and last session he was ever willing to answer questions regarding the affair. To this day, he still gets reactive if the affair is brought up.

One positive outcome I did help them develop was for her to be able to say, "I am in a dark place right now," when she felt hurt or triggered going forward. She wasn't allowed to go into the content beyond that with Dennis, but he was willing to be coached into replying, "Do you need anything from me right now?" While talking about the details of the affair was off limits, this coached conversation still helped them to support each other in future times when she was struggling.

Your Human Self

One of the challenges in therapy can be how to navigate lies. In many therapy situations, I find myself feeling overwhelmed when I know that the client in my office is currently lying to their partner. As you do more of this work, it becomes very easy to identify lying. You will notice very small details that change in the client when they lie. They may avert their eyes or a small part of their forehead scrunches when they tell the lie. What do you do when you think a partner is lying?

One of the things that has helped me work through this process is to have fellow clinicians I can share stories with about my challenges in therapy. No matter how long I have been a therapist, there are still ways I can learn and grow clinically. It helps to hear how other clinicians work through these situations, especially if anything feels too close to home.

I think it is common for clinicians to struggle with feeling responsible for the choices their clients make at times. While this struggle is normal, it can be helpful to have a personal mantra or reminder that you aren't responsible. We are responsible for guiding clients in making better decisions, but ultimately they are responsible for what they do with this information. I have called clients out at times (in an individual session) and discussed my concerns that they are still lying about the other relationship. I have also been more covert and suggested that it is common for someone to struggle with letting go of that old relationship. No matter which approach I have used, there are still clients who have chosen to lie.

When these things occur, I try to remind myself that I am doing the best I can with the situation. I sometimes will ask my husband for encouragement or a fellow therapist for the same. Ultimately, we want to help our clients live happy and healthy lives. It is hard to see them make choices that can damage their relationships.

Sometimes the only thing that really helps is to have a mantra I repeat to myself. A common one that is used in AA is the serenity prayer. Whether you are religious or not, the message behind these words can be a good reminder to any person. A paraphrased version can go like this: "God," "earth," or "my own sense of higher self," grant to me serenity to accept the things I cannot change, courage to change the things I can, and wisdom to know the difference (Anonymous, 2013).

Milestone 4   Choosing to Stay or Leave

How common is it for people to work on their relationship? Is cheating normal? Can couple relationships that start in an affair end up together? How does someone decide whether to put effort into the relationship or move on? These questions are just a few of the many questions your clients will ask you when they start therapy. In this chapter, I would like to offer some guidance for how to help your clients figure out their best course of action.

There are many factors that a person should consider. Was it a one-time affair or is it one infidelity in a string of many indiscretions? Most individuals are not chronic cheaters. However, there are a couple of personality types that do tend to cheat more often than others. In this first part of the chapter, I will cover these personality types so you can help your clients begin to assess if their partner made a mistake or if there is a serious issue that could hurt the relationship. After this, I will offer some intervention styles that can be helpful in cases where a person made a mistake and does not have a global personality disorder.

Personality Types that Lead to Cheating

After finding out about his wife's long-term relationship, John came to therapy to answer his own questions. He had increasingly thought his wife Gina had been deceiving him. She would make excuses about needing to work late or getting to work early to finish a project. One day he decided to follow her secretly, only to see her pull into an apartment parking lot and walk into a man's apartment. He confronted her about the cheating and found out she had engaged in the affair for over six months. He was heartbroken sitting in the therapy chair. He asked a million questions. Could he ever fully trust her again? How could he know if she would cheat or not? How could she lie to him for all this time? Sadly, there were no easy answers.

These are questions many people have to grapple with after an affair. I hear many more questions that make perfect sense. Once someone is a cheater will they always be a cheater? Is my partner a sociopath? If not, how could they lie to me and not feel guilty? Did they ever feel guilty? How can I be sure this will never happen again?

There are many reasons why a person may cheat. Some of the most common include opportunity, having a higher mate value (or essentially being very good looking), having a job or a partner in a job who travels often (Estroff Marano, 2012), having a very high sex drive that is not satisfied in a current relationship, and some personality types.

The most common personality types that have been linked to cheating include people with psychopathic or Machiavellian personality traits (Author Unknown, Truth about Deception, 2014). However, these are not specific diagnoses that exist in the DSM-V. A psychopath is defined as having the following symptoms: superficial charm, pathological lying, inflated sense of self-worth, being manipulative or conning others, impulsiveness, irresponsibility, lacking empathy, and criminal acts in several realms (Tracy, 2016). This is not a personality disorder that exists in the DSM-V but it could easily be related to anti-social personality disorder or narcissistic personality disorder (American Psychiatric Association, 2013). The diagnosis of unspecified, disruptive, impulse control and conduct disorder could also be related to the term "psychopathy". The trouble with "psychopathy" is that it is more of a pop psychology term or an umbrella term that is meant to cover a wide range of potential diagnoses. It also tends to be used more in law enforcement as a way to describe people.

The Machiavellian personality style includes being a master manipulator, and is also commonly associated with infidelity. They are very deceptive and tend to be duplicitous in nature. You may see some of the following symptoms: emotional detachment and a cynical outlook on life; the use of tactics such as charm, friendliness, self-disclosure, guilt, and pressure; the use of other people as stepping stones to meet their ultimate goal (Hartley, 2015). This term is also not listed in the DSM-V. People with this personality type are commonly in positions of power. If we were to try and connect this personality type to a DSM-V diagnosis, we could potentially link to any of the previous diagnoses discussed under psychopathy. I would also include borderline personality disorder in this mix because people with this diagnosis are commonly seen as being manipulative. Of course, as a clinician you need to explore the symptoms of the person over time and see how closely they fit with the DSM-V definitions before suggesting a diagnosis.

While these personality types are commonly linked with chronic infidelity, not every client who has committed an affair can be classified as either personality type. The reality is that the statistics for cheating/infidelity are high among the general population as well. With the growing number of avenues by which people can cheat (i.e., Facebook, Snapchat, dating websites such as Ashley Madison, etc.), it is getting harder to assume there must be something inherently broken about the client who does step outside their relationship.

In fact, one of the most common stories I hear in my practice looks like this one: a married couple in their forties; the partners have not had many partners prior to their marriage; a death of a parent or loved one occurred within the last two to three years; the grief from the loss turned into a longer depression for one partner; the depressed partner begins to get restless and seek something more in their life, asking the question, "Is this all there is to my life?"; the depressed partner starts to commiserate with someone in their close proximity (a friend or co-worker) who is also feeling some depression or restlessness. This commiseration turns into something more.

I cannot begin to tell you how often a couple describes the scenario above to me after someone has committed an affair. The minor details change here and there, but the bigger commonality is startling. These depressed clients are not necessarily narcissists or psychopaths. I think it is pretty common for people struggling with depression to either lash out or look for something to fill the void. They need something in their life to feel better, and they don't always have the best outlet. There is also some naivete that the cheating partner may hold prior to the relationship. If you ask them if they ever thought they would have cheated, they will answer a firm no. Yet, they are in your office because they recently cheated.

Honestly, when I see naivete on either side, I strongly encourage a shift in attitude for my clients. I truly believe that anyone is capable of making a mistake and cheating. We are not perfect people and we can all fall. With this viewpoint, I think couples look at situations with more discernment after an infidelity has occurred. It is better to take responsibility for your ability to hurt your partner and then to take actions going forward to hold yourself accountable. For example, the attitude shift looks like this,

> Anyone could make a mistake, including me. I am aware of this possibility now. From here on out, I will take actions to hold myself accountable. I will consciously look for potential risks and do things to protect my relationship. I will not just hope for the best or expect my partner to blindly trust me.

This mindset does help put some clients at ease because there is more responsibility taken. However, there are no guarantees in this world. Regardless of what plans are in place, couples must understand that it is possible for anyone to make a mistake. No person nor therapist can guarantee that an infidelity will never occur in the future.

Helpful Interventions

In this next section, I will cover a few techniques that can help your clients get closer to finding answers. The hard part about being the therapist is that we can guide people but we cannot ultimately make the decisions. The clients we work with ultimately have to deal with the consequences of their actions, so it is their job to make the best decisions for themselves and for us to support them through the process.

Knock 'em Off the Fence

Many clients struggle with whether to end or stay in a relationship. One helpful strategy for helping a couple to work through this is a variation of a skill from motivational interviewing. In motivational interviewing, there are five stages of change to assess for in your client: pre-contemplative, contemplative, preparation, action, and relapse prevention (Norcross et al., 2011). Usually clients who are struggling with the question "should I stay or should I go?" are in the pre-contemplation stage or the contemplation stage of change. They are willing to talk to someone about the issues, but they are on the fence about what to do next.

After an infidelity, many clients can stay a long time on top of that fence without moving forward. The problem with staying on the fence is that it causes two separate problems. On the one hand, it can prevent clients from doing positive things to fix their marriage/partnership. It can also easily keep individuals from taking active steps towards ending a marriage/partnership.

The skill I use to help is to knock them off the fence "figuratively." I tell the couple why they should not be together and make a very specific recommendation for them to end their relationship. I then go into various reasons why they should end it using their very words and language. "You said it yourself, he never listens to you. You are often alone as a mother and nothing will change. You are right. Nothing will change and you should divorce him." The language is meant to be jarring, hard to hear, and to restate most of the reasons they have already told you that they shouldn't be together.

Before using this skill, the therapist must explain very clearly what they are about to do and why. This is important because many couples value our advice. If you tell them to leave each other without explaining it is a strategy, they will be forced to either end their relationship or end therapy with you because they do not trust your judgment for their relationship.

Essentially, I tell the couple I am going to knock them off the fence on purpose. The reason is to force them to feel what it would be like to potentially lose their partner. I explain to the couple that this is a very risky strategy, but it can also be a helpful one. It is risky because sometimes when a person is told to leave their partner, they feel relief. In some cases, a client needed permission to end an already dying relationship. If that isn't what the couple hoped for from therapy, that risk can be very painful. However, this strategy can also have the opposite effect. When someone is forced to deeply consider what it would feel like to lose their partner, they are reminded of all the good there still is in the relationship. This gives them a deeper motivation to work in therapy.

This skill is not for every couple. I use it solely for couples who may potentially have something to work out but are struggling with the ultimate question, "Should I stay or should I go?" I would not use this skill for a couple that is abusive towards each other. In domestic violence cases, there can be a risk of harm to either one or both partners. A definitive intervention like this could easily escalate.

Affair Proofing

Most of your couples want you to talk about affair proofing the marriage at some point. An affair is essentially one of the worst things that can happen for most people. When they come to therapy, they want to know for certain they will never have to deal with this again. How do we actually do this successfully?

First of all, I believe in setting realistic expectations. There is no guarantee in life or easy predictor for someone's future behavior. In fact, past behaviors are the easiest evidence to draw from for predicting future behavior. Since the past behavior is an infidelity, you will find both partners struggling with trusting themselves and being able to trust that their partner won't cheat again.

The way I address this is to be very practical with clients. I state that each person is capable of making huge mistakes. The reality is that people who have an over-inflated view of themselves tend to be the ones to fall the hardest. In my clinical practice, it is very common for the client who cheated to have said many times in their life prior to the infidelity, "I would never cheat! I don't understand how someone could make a decision like this. If I were ever thinking about cheating, I would just leave my husband." The wild thing is they rarely do this. The people who say this are often the very people who cheat, who stay with their partners, and who want to work to save their marriages.

This skill's first step is to help your clients admit they have a dark side – that they are capable of not only cheating, but hurting each other, neglecting each other's needs, and even at times being emotionally or in some cases physically abusive. The first step to prevention is ownership. We have to accept the reality that people hurt each other every day and no one is above it all. Another way to put this is, every person has flaws. You are trying to help each individual accept that they are not flawless.

When I can help each partner to begin to accept this part of themselves, then I can move on to the next step, which is identifying vulnerabilities that lead to cheating for the population and for themselves personally. In her article "From Promise to Promiscuity," Hara Estroff Marano (2012) described several common features that make it easier for people to cheat. These include: opportunity; higher levels of income; lots of travel away from home; professions that include macho culture (male dominated, acceptance of promiscuity); lack of social connections; friendships that are accepting of cheating behaviors; partners who tend to be very private and lack general openness; insecurity and low self-esteem; alcohol. These are various factors or vulnerabilities that can lead to cheating if they are not kept in check. Not every client will struggle with each factor. However, knowing the factors can help clients begin to identify their personal vulnerabilities for cheating.

For example, I had a client, John, who worked as a physical therapist. He cheated with a girl that he was working with. When we explored the various potential vulnerabilities that could have led to his cheating he could point to a few. First, he has always suffered from low self-esteem. He deeply believed no one could ever find him attractive and was surprised even when his current wife found him attractive. When his co-worker showed interest, it made him feel handsome and as though he had some worth. Another vulnerability of his was his best friend Larry. Larry has always been single, dating, and never committed to any one person. Often when he hung out with Larry, he would see Larry cheat on his partners. Larry encompassed a "Bros before Hos" mentality and was even willing to keep secrets for his friend about his whereabouts. Identifying a client's vulnerabilities is the responsibility of your client. You can help them by giving these common reasons people justify cheating, but it is ultimately their job to explore the ways they justified their own behaviors.

I actually encourage both partners to go through this process for themselves. Even though the hurt partner has not committed an infidelity, many people have vulnerabilities that could lead them to commit an infidelity in the future. A hurt partner, for example, can become vulnerable because they have been cheated on. As a result, they are at some risk of committing an infidelity out of spite. I have found that when you have the couple work through this process as a team, the unfaithful partner does not feel as blamed in therapy.

The final step is to help each partner to begin to set up ways to keep themselves accountable through these vulnerabilities. In this process, it can be very eye opening for the unfaithful partner to see the many ways that the hurt partner has already been setting these boundaries to protect the relationship. For example, Charity and Wendy were in treatment because Charity had been unfaithful one night when out with friends at a bar. As we discussed ways they could hold themselves accountable, Wendy stated that she always asks a friend (typically the designated driver) to keep an eye on her when she drinks. She recognizes that she makes impulsive decisions while drinking. She will ask this friend to gently encourage them to leave situations that may be risky. Charity had no idea that Wendy had set up this accountability for herself. Charity did not have any type of accountability when she drank. This posed a risk especially during nights when she drank in excess.

There are many ways to help clients set up accountability or set boundaries around behaviors. For example, if a person has used the phone to cheat, they can agree to keep their phone out in a public place when they get home. If a person travels a lot, they can invite their partner along to some of their trips or always extend an open invitation for their partner to come to different locations they travel to as a sort of accountability. In some cases, partners have decided that travel is too risky for them and they work towards finding a job that keeps them closer to home for longer.

The key to this process is to help clients be flexible and creative without imposing a "Big Brother" mentality. In the short-term, doing a lot of checking up on each other is somewhat normal because trust has recently been broken. Long-term, this type of checking up behavior will cause fights and more trouble in the relationship. The hurt partner will say, "I don't want to live in a relationship in which I have to check up on my partner." The unfaithful partner will say, "I don't want to feel like he/she is constantly checking up on me. I still want to be able to live my life." The best way to combat this for your clients is to teach them to hold themselves accountable and to choose the ways they personally need to protect the relationship. This helps each person feel autonomy, while also helping them to intentionally set up ways to prevent affairs from occurring in the future.

Finally, I always set a realistic expectation. Never assume that this could not happen in the future. Essentially, couples need to do two things consistently to prevent affairs. (1) Always work on creating an awesome relationship that makes other people jealous. When you have a great relationship, you are motivated to protect it. (2) Own the fact that you can make a mistake at any point and regularly find ways to address these vulnerabilities honestly as a team.

Official Separation

Many couples consider taking a separation after someone has an affair. The after effects are painful and the couple finds themselves arguing constantly with no positive endings. Personally, I have no positive or negative beliefs about taking a separation, but I do want to share some statistics. Approximately 87 percent of couples who separate eventually end up divorcing, while the other 13 percent eventually reconcile (Divorce Statistics Website, 2016). Just looking at the figures, the odds point to sticking together rather than separating. However, this statistic does not take into account people who are trying separation in a more therapeutic way. Some couples just leave each other and wait to see if things change.

Whenever I talk about a separation with my couples, I always offer the pros and cons of making a decision like this. I also don't tell a couple firmly that they must separate. This is an option, and it is usually brought up by the couple first, not by me. However, I have had a few couples in which I was concerned about violence or the effect their fighting had on their children. In some of these situations, I did very seriously suggest separation as an option for safety. The most important thing you need to remember as a therapist is that your words do affect the decisions a couple makes regarding their relationship. Anytime you suggest something extreme, always offer options and make them aware of the risks.

Here are some of the pros and cons to a trial separation. On the one hand, absence sometimes makes the heart grow fonder. When people have to live apart, they sometimes realize how much they depend on their partner for different things. The hope is that this separation helps them to miss their partner and get close again. On the other hand, a separation can also help one or more partners feel confident that they don't need a partner anymore. Actually, they could be just fine without them. Each outcome is possible. Without very clear boundaries and understanding about how to have the separation, there could also be misunderstandings about what is acceptable behavior during the separation.

The next step I take is to outline some guidelines for how to take an effective separation. While these are not set in stone, they do seem to help my couples decide how to proceed.

1   Set a timeline for how long to separate. I usually suggest that couples take a two-month period to separate. If possible, I prefer my couples not to make any big life changes, such as getting an apartment or leaving the state. This two-month period is to really focus on the marriage, while also getting some time away from each other for clarity.
2   Define the purpose of the separation. If the purpose is to see if they can work things out, then every rule for the separation should be in line with that end goal. For example, no one should be allowed to date other people, because that would be counter to the goal of getting back together. If the purpose ultimately is to break it to the partner that they want a divorce, then the couple should be honest and start making that transition.
3   Set very clear expectations. I suggest that couples have weekly therapy as a couple and also see their own individual therapists. I also encourage them to set weekly date nights and a weekly relationship check in time where they talk through some of their issues outside of therapy. I tell couples to only see each other during these times and to really try to give their partner freedom in these other times, except for as needed to co-parent. Firmly – no dating other people allowed!
4   At the end of the agreed upon time frame, come back and re-evaluate the situation. Have they gotten any closer to an end goal? Do they want to make things work? Are they still wanting to end things? At this point, I help the couple make decisions for the long-term.

In any case, trial separations have some risks. You cannot know people's motivations altogether. Sometimes, a partner is requesting a separation so they have freedom to see their lover. If you notice these things occurring, you can directly call the partner out in an individual session, but the reality is that we cannot control our clients. Do your best to be honest and upfront about what you think is best, and then understand that you have to let it go if couples end up doing what they want regardless of your best advice.

A Good Story

Kevin and Becky came into therapy after Kevin had cheated on her. For about ten years, their marriage had been a sexless marriage. Each of them had grown apart in different ways, and at the point Kevin met Donica, he thought his marriage was already over. Kevin admitted he did not love Donica. He always loved his wife Becky, but she never showed interest in sex with him and he got very lonely. In their first session, they were both unsure whether or not they could work to improve things. Becky was very worried that if she tried, she would just end up getting hurt again.

It struck me that they both were very quiet personalities and did not like confrontation. I probed some about why they felt their sex life had started to wane over time. Over the years, they stopped initiating sex with one another because they often did not want to inconvenience the other person. One person might slightly mention they had a rough day, so the other would avoid the topic of sex, assuming that this would bother their partner. On other days, one might be busy with the kids. Again, the other would not bring up sex because they did not want to inconvenience their partner. Over time, they each had started to build separate lives.

The longer things went between sex, the more Kevin would find other activities to occupy his time. Becky was never one to tell him no, and would encourage him to engage in activities he might enjoy. I asked them a silly question on purpose, "You know you both are just way too nice? It sounds like each of you was so concerned about inconveniencing the other person, that you lost your sex life!" They both agreed. Even when Kevin described the affair he had with Donica, it was often coupled with drinking and a lot of shame. He stated he never really wanted to be with anyone else but Becky. After they would go through long periods without sex, he had assumed she no longer loved him. She assured him she did want to have sex with him. However, she also struggled to initiate sex because she had never felt very comfortable being the initiator. There were many times she might have been interested but too scared to say or do anything.

During the course of our work together, I counseled Becky in ways that she could practice being more assertive about her sexual needs. In addition, I also counseled Kevin to initiate with her even if he was worried she might not be interested. In many ways, he was rejecting himself without giving her a chance to show interest. In addition, we did a lot of work around building trust and helping them open up about the pain the affair caused. Becky was honestly more mature than most about how she worked through the affair. Towards the end of therapy, they had shared many of their secrets and even some sexual fantasies they wanted to try with each other. They both reported they felt much closer and more in love than they had ever been before. It took a lot of honesty and letting go of old habits.

A Bad Story

Beverly and Brian came into session because Beverly had recently committed an affair with another man, John. During their first session, Beverly appeared only partially committed to the process of therapy. She would use non-committal language such as "I just don't know what I want"; "I have not been happy for a long time"; "I'm very confused about things." While this type of language can be common for a person after they have committed infidelity, it may also be an indicator that a client is still having the affair. Brian's language was very committal. He stated things like, "I want to spend the rest of my life with her"; "I am willing to do whatever it takes"; "I have never loved anyone more than Beverly."

I split this couple up into two individual sessions to help each of them figure out what was going on. I was up front with Beverly, and told her it sounded like she was still talking to John or even still in a relationship with him. She admitted she had not stopped talking with him and was considering moving into an apartment with him. However, she was unsure if it was the best choice. She and Brian had a daughter, Sophie. She did not want to hurt Sophie, who was only 12.

The hard part about doing this work is you as a therapist have to find a way to help people make a decision about their next step. Often these decisions appear to be lose–lose – in either choice you lose something or hurt someone. Staying in the gray zone does not help the situation. I told Beverly that she would need to pick a path one way or the other and just jump in. I stated the truth of the matter is that there would be pros and cons to choosing either partner. Staying with her husband, there would be a lot of work done to improve the situation. Many couples go through ups and downs and can take years to work through the affair fully. On the opposite side, if she chose John, she would be starting over from scratch and there would be many challenges. It would split her family apart and relationships that start as affairs tend to have a lot of trust issues going forward.

Beverly just could not choose any side; therefore, she dropped out of therapy and continued in both relationships – the gray zone. Brian chose to stay in therapy individually because he knew he needed help figuring out how to handle the situation. He continued in therapy individually for the next year. For the entire year, his wife stayed in both relationships. She would spend a few weeks trying things with Brian and then find herself going back to John. This year was tortuous for Brian. I tried to offer him support, offer suggestions to help him put his foot down with Beverly, and tried to guide him towards improving himself.

Eventually Beverly chose to stay in her marriage and around this time Brian quit coming to therapy. It was a long grueling year trying to help Brian figure out what to do with his life. After seeing him individually for so long, I suggested that they do counseling as a couple together with someone else so they could get a fresh start. In this scenario, I tried to guide the best I could, but Beverly had her own choices to make and felt guilty coming to therapy when she could not make a choice. In a case like this, you have to do your best but understand that you cannot control the choices your clients will make.

Your Human Self

It can be very hard to work with couples who are perpetually in the unknown category of treatment – meaning they are constantly asking the question of whether they should stay or leave the relationship. It is difficult for us because, based on which decision they make, we can guide them in different paths. Motivational interviewing techniques are usually the most helpful when people are on the fence, but it can still feel very exhausting to see people not getting closer to an end result after months of therapy.

First off, it's important for you to remember that after an affair, it is common for your couples to still be asking this question years later. Some will struggle with whether or not they made the right decision. Some other people never figure it out. As much as we try to guide them in a direction, they will still feel disillusioned at times. What you need to ask yourself is, "Do I still have the strength to offer a non-partial, middle ground approach, or am I getting to the point of frustration?" If you find yourself getting increasingly frustrated, it is okay to suggest your clients either start working in individual counseling or even refer them to a new therapist who can offer a fresh perspective.

You could honestly spend years saying similar things to the same clients. "What do you think is the best path for you?" or "You've committed to your partner for now, how can you make the most of the relationship that you have and close the door on the past?" If you find yourself losing your compassion or sense being non-partial, be honest with yourself. You are only hurting yourself by keeping clients that frustrate you.

Also, not in every case do you need to terminate. Sometimes the real issue is that you have not been taking care of yourself. Working with this population is a very challenging job and requires many months of taxing and emotionally painful work. If you struggle with self-care, here are some tips for supporting yourself so you can be there for your clients:

1   Get a massage;
2   Take a long, luxurious bath with candles and soft music;
3   Spend a night out with friends – no talking about stress, just have fun;

4   Connect with relationships that are permanent – this can be a helpful reminder that not all relationships end.

Whatever you do, make sure you have a regular self-care routine. Don't wait until you are sick of everything and everyone to take care of yourself or you will burn out.

Milestone 5   Repairing Unresolved Issues in the Relationship

When it comes to affair treatment, there is a lot at stake for the couple. One of the first issues you have to address is what problems existed in the relationship prior to the infidelity. Couples who come into therapy could have suffered with chronic depression, long-term addictions, and coping with a sexless marriage.

As their therapist, your role is to assess for any problems that may or may not have occurred during the relationship. One challenge with this issue is that not every couple had problems prior to an infidelity. In her article "From Promise to Promiscuity," Hara Estroff Marano (2012) describes how it can be very confusing for a couple to experience the pain of an infidelity when the marriage was a happy one. Instead of assuming that a marriage was doomed from the start, it can be helpful to look at more contextual factors that may contribute to the infidelity, such as having more opportunity, or being involved in situations that deplete self-control, such as exposure to alcohol, high levels of travel for work, and having a stressful job.

It can actually be a harder job to work on things if the marriage was happy because you will find the hurt partner searching for answers to what went wrong in the relationship. For example, Jemma and Aaron came into therapy after she found out he committed a four-year affair with another man. The affair started when he met a man that was very outgoing and pursued him sexually. He had never really thought of himself as bisexual. However, his wife's travel schedule with work left many open times for him to be alone and to experiment.

Now that they were seeking treatment, Jemma was afraid not only that something might be wrong in the relationship, but that Aaron was gay and really should not be in this relationship. The two had met at a very young age and only dated each other. When she asked him repeatedly what went wrong, he always stated she was perfect and she did nothing wrong. He also stated he had been unsure about his sexuality and this affair offered him the opportunity to explore his bisexual interests. As he continued to explore, he had recently broken off the relationship because he realized he cared more about his marriage than he cared for this sexual relationship.

His partner found out after the other man tried to reach out to Aaron again after their break up.

As a clinician, you have to be open to the idea that really the only thing that was wrong with the relationship was the affair. It is common for the unfaithful partner to pull away from their spouse while they have an affair for a variety of reasons. They may feel incredible guilt and avoid their partner to avoid this extreme guilt. They may grow closer sexually and emotionally to the other person, which often causes them to distance from their spouse. One statement I use often with clients is a play on the words of Abraham Lincoln, "A heart divided cannot stand." Essentially, once a person starts investing in the new relationship, they lose investment in the older one. This same thing can happen after they recommit to their old relationship and agree to let go of the affair relationship. Once they have grieved the loss of the affair and totally commit to their spouse, you will see some partners look back on the affair partner in disgust or disdain. (This only happens if they completely give up the affair and fully invest back in their current relationship.) As their clinician, you need to spend a good deal of time assessing the relationship, both in its current state and prior to the affair. If they both agree that things were good, then your job is to help them rebuild trust and get back to that positive place again.

However, if there were chronic unresolved issues, it can be helpful to explore these in therapy. I usually try to take at least one session individually with each client to explore unresolved issues. I use this time to assess for any mental health issues, communication issues, and/or substance abuse issues. I also look for medical problems that could contribute to stress on the marriage. For example, a chronic pain condition, cancer, or a debilitating disease that they struggled to work through can commonly be the start of distancing in a marriage. Another common occurrence is to have an unfaithful spouse who recently experienced a great loss such as a death of a loved one. It is not that the death caused the affair, but the unresolved grief might have led the partner to begin commiserating with someone other than their spouse.

Once you have done a full assessment of the clients' issues, it is very important to offer a treatment plan that helps the couple work through these issues as a team, so their marriage can be stronger going forward. The timing of this work can be crucial to how you build trust with your clients. Even if there were problems prior to an infidelity, if you move to work on these too quickly, the hurt spouse will feel as though you are neglecting the bigger issue of working through the affair. In the same regard, if you only focus on the affair, the unfaithful partner will begin to feel alienated and neglected because you are avoiding the bigger issues of the relationship that they feel led them to the affair. One way I handle this is to first work the couple through any initial crisis. After this, I will do test sessions, where we begin to cover the bigger issues. If the hurt partner responds well, I may continue to go back and forth between trust issues and bigger problems. If the hurt partner responds poorly, I reassure them that we will get back to the marriage problems after we have settled some of the initial crisis points.

Interventions

In this section, I discuss several interventions that are aimed at helping the couple work together to improve their marriage. It can be tough to convince couples to do this. Often the hurt partner wants the unfaithful partner to take most of the blame. For a time, the unfaithful partner may take on the blame. Over time, if this interaction pattern is not shifted, the unfaithful partner will get tired of therapy and possibly drop out. These interventions are aimed at helping shift this cycle.

Cleaning Up the Marriage as a Team

One of the hardest jobs you have as a therapist will be to convince the couple to work as a team to solve their relationship issues. After an infidelity, the hurt partner can get angry if you try to suggest that there might be things they each need to work on. If certain things are not addressed in therapy, then the unfaithful partner may feel as though they are still dealing with the very problems that led to the affair.

You have to be delicate with this matter. One way I accomplish this is by explaining that I am a systems therapist who tries to understand how couples interact with one another. A systems therapist does not see each individual in the relationship as separate but as a part of a much bigger system. One of the main focuses in systems theory is to look at the patterns of behavior in the relationship (Nichols & Schwartz, 2006). I explain this to clients by discussing a typical argument. Here is an example:

> Usually in an argument, a person doesn't yell at themselves. Instead one person says something and this escalates the other person's defenses. Then that person says something to escalate the situation further. As an argument progresses, each person plays a part in making the situation worse.

There has been some criticism of systems theory in that it can put unnecessary blame on people who really have done nothing wrong. An infidelity is a perfect example of how systems theory could potentially cause someone to feel blamed. Here is an example:

> First you started avoiding sex. Then he started to feel rejected and talk more to his co-workers. Then, when you noticed him withdraw you began to yell at him more for not coming home on time. This distanced

him further and he started to flirt and hang out with one co-worker on a regular basis.

One very important thing to explain to couples facing infidelity is that while there are systems that were in place prior to the affair that may need some examining, there is only one person who is responsible for making the decision to actually cheat. At any given point before the infidelity occurred, that partner could have suggested they seek counseling, asked for a separation to figure things out, or even suggested divorce if the relationship were not improved somehow.

Another thing I explain is that while one person may have stepped out of the relationship, it is still a mess they both have to clean up as a team. When I say this, I try to acknowledge the anger the hurt partner may be feeling at having to clean up a mess they didn't create. I acknowledge the pain they suffer as a result of feeling like a stranger in their own marriage suddenly. I encourage them for every step they take to work through those old problems.

Essentially, this intervention is a version of the both/and approach in DBT (Linehan, 1993). The both/and approach simply states that you try to be accepting and validating of the challenge the client is facing, while also encouraging change. "I can see why this would be difficult for you and you have to work together to make the situation better." It uses the term "and" because it helps the message come across more respectfully and less aggressive than a "but" might come across. When clients hear the term "but" it is as though they completely stop hearing the validation and only hear a criticism.

What Is a Good Marriage?

Long ago, therapists used to think that if you work on communication, you will resolve most issues as a couple. However, Gottman and Silver's (2015) book shows that couples need a few things to have a good relationship. These traits include: being good friends and knowing each other well; nurturing fondness and admiration; turning towards each other; being influenced by your partner; solving solvable problems; overcoming gridlock; creating shared meaning. I won't be able to cover each of these principles in detail. However, it is important for you to read as much information as possible about what it takes to create a healthy marriage. The book, *The Seven Principles for Making Marriage Work*, by Gottman and Silver covers these principles and is based in 20 years of research on couples.

In their book, Gottman and Silver discuss something called a love map. Essentially a love map is the way in which couples learn deeply about their partner's inner life. The more we know about each other, the easier it is to feel connected and loved. To be a good friend, you need to care about your partner's life and what matters to them. This includes asking open ended questions and developing a healthy curiosity about their inner world. I tell couples they don't know each other as much as they think they do because people's interests and lives change over time.

Daniel and George had been in therapy for a while. They were finally getting past that initial crisis phase and were now working on the relationship. I started to ask Daniel a question, when George jumped in and said, "I already know what he is going to say." I moved to George and said, "What do you think he will say?" George replied, "That I am never home enough and he is tired of being alone." I asked Daniel if that was what he had planned to say. Daniel replied, "No. I was going to say I understand that he has to work sometimes. I also understand that he cares about his position. I don't want to stand in his work's way. I just want to be prioritized too."

Many times, couples don't know each other as well after they have been arguing or distant for a time. I often find that after an affair, my couples have a lot to learn about each other. Some of them were just going through the motions and rarely cared to ask about their partner's lives.

Being a good friend entails a lot. It involves spending time together, learning about your partner's life, being caring, and being receptive to change. It also includes giving as well as receiving. When you are working with your couples, it is important to not only get them past the crisis but to get their relationship back in working order. They need to feel as though they share many positive experiences and can count on each other. If they don't get to this point, the affair will start to be the end of the relationship.

Individualizing Care

No matter what couple comes into your therapy room, there is no one-size-fits-all strategy for helping your couples overcome infidelity. A big part of our job is to not only help couples figure out the infidelity, but also to work on their individual issues. It's common for someone to come into therapy with me for one issue only to reveal other issues they also need to address.

It used to be assumed that anyone who engaged in an affair had a relationship problem that needed to be solved. However, as Estroff Marano (2012) pointed out, there are couples who experience infidelity during times that were fine or even happy. This is what can make the situation very confusing. As a therapist you may also assume that there is some bigger issue to deal with, when the reality is that one person made a mistake that is now causing issues.

We need to look at the big picture and listen to what was going on before and after the affair in the relationship. If the couple describes a marriage that was perfectly happy, then you need to individualize the care to help them focus on relapse prevention. If there were problems, these need to be addressed in order for your couple to be whole again as a couple.

One of the ways I explain this process to clients is by stating that I take a holistic approach to counseling. I explain that my goal is to help them in all aspects of their marriage. This can include parenting, finances, sex, individual issues, and the infidelity. When couples understand this coming in, it makes it easier to assess in multiple areas of the relationship.

There can be many ways you may need to individualize your care. I would look for individual mental health diagnoses, problems with drugs or alcohol, and problems in the greater system.

A Good Story

Joline and Terrence came into therapy because Joline had an emotional affair with a high school sweetheart. As they told their back story, Terrence had confessed to having been a porn addict over a year ago. During this time, he worked tirelessly to help improve his addiction. He realized his porn usage kept him from seeking out real intimacy with his wife. It was during his treatment that Joline started to rely on her high school sweetheart as a friend. As Terrence got better, Joline fell further into the other relationship.

Now they were here to work on their relationship and put things back together. I asked about their home life and the kids. They both reported having very different values about parenting. He took a very laid-back approach, which made her become stricter and more controlling. Now that they were working on things, they wanted to be on the same page, but they were struggling with parenting as a team. Joline admitted that when their parenting issues got out of hand, she tended to seek solace from the other man.

In addition to infidelity work, I encouraged them to focus on developing co-parenting skills. They both agreed that this had been a point of contention for quite some time and that they needed to find a way to feel like partners. We started by setting up some family rules. One thing they valued was being able to agree upon some of the rules and understand each other. I suggested they include their kids in making up the family rules so they would be just as motivated to follow the rules.

We continued to work on both issues going back and forth. One session would focus on trust building while the next session would focus on strategies for them to work better as parents. By the end of therapy, they had developed some family rules and come up with consequences that their kids agreed to follow (for the most part). In addition, they were having regular family meetings with their kids and individually as a couple outside of therapy to fine tune issues and improve the situation. Both of them had gotten better about recognizing their challenges as parents. Instead of criticizing each other, they were encouraging each other.

A Bad Story

A few years back, I had Olivia come into therapy by herself because she was trying to get over her husband's infidelity. It had happened over a year ago. Her husband was a DJ and often hung out in bars and nightclubs during the evenings. One night, he got too drunk and started flirting with a girl at the bar. They ended up going home together and having a one-night stand. Olivia found out about the situation after one of their mutual friends sent pictures of her husband with the girl that night. She confronted him about the situation, he confessed and said it would never happen again.

Now, a year later, Olivia was still struggling with getting over the affair. Her partner was tired of hearing her talk about it and wanted the whole thing to go away. She stated that the main goal was to put the situation behind her once and for all. As we worked together, I asked her what things they had done to rebuild trust since the affair. She stated not much had happened. He was only willing to talk about the situation for about a month and then the conversation started getting defensive from that point on.

After assessing for different challenges going on in the relationship, I started to realize that there were other issues. Their conflicts in general were pretty intense and really no work had been done after the affair to really reassure Olivia about what had happened. Her partner expected her to trust him, blindly, that he would never do it again, and he was not willing to do much else. She was essentially in therapy because she had a partner who was unwilling to help her get over the situation.

I asked her if her partner knew she was in therapy. She replied that he was aware she was in therapy. Honestly, I really wanted him to come into therapy to see if he would be willing to work on the relationship now. While I felt I could give her coping techniques, I worried that she was at risk of being hurt going forward if the partner never at least tried to improve the situation or rebuild trust. Olivia stated she would try to see if her partner would come into therapy.

After a few weeks of individual sessions, Olivia stated she would be able to bring her partner Cornell into therapy, but he only committed to one session. He stated he would not be willing to do anything beyond this session. This felt like both a win and a loss, because I really believed that clinically it would be more helpful if they approached couples issues together as a team. I hoped long-term their relationship could become stronger.

That next week, Cornell came into session. You could tell by his demeanor that he did not want to be there, but he was trying to tolerate the situation to make his wife happy. I asked him what he wanted out of the session. He replied that he was only here to support his wife for this session. I did my best to state my case that if Cornell really wanted to help

Olivia get over the infidelity, it would be most helpful if they both worked on building trust and improving the relationship. Many times, an infidelity can be an opportunity to revamp a relationship that has been struggling. He was able to admit they had been struggling with conflict both prior to, and especially after, the infidelity. He still was unwilling to commit to therapy. He didn't believe therapy was helpful but he was fine with his partner going if she needed it.

I used the session to ask him questions and learn more about his situation. Then I made sure to explain what kinds of strategies they could use as a couple to improve the relationship. I suggested he take some time to consider what we discussed to see if he might be willing to change his position on things.

That next week, Olivia came in by herself and explained that Cornell considered the information but did not want to pursue therapy at this time. While I could tell this was a hard blow for Olivia, I was at least glad we had a small chance to try and help them improve their relationship. I reassured her that even as an individual working in therapy, she can affect change in her relationship. Therapy from that point on focused on building pro-social relationship skills and helping her to find ways to reduce the hurt she continued to experience as a result of the infidelity.

Your Human Self

When we do this work, it can really make us question the quality of our own relationships as a therapist. As a part of our daily work, we are teaching people to have better relationships. Every day we teach couples new tools and skills and guide them in being better people. This can be a challenge when you go home and get into an argument/conflict with your partner. Day-to-day, we all go through various challenges regardless of whether we know the skills. How do you as a therapist handle this struggle?

I think an important step for all therapists to take is to admit that while we know many skills, that does NOT mean we know how to have the perfect marriage. Relationship skills can be very hard to put into practice. I think it makes it more difficult for us to know what the "right step" is to take. For example, in one of my podcasts, I interviewed a fellow sex therapist about how arguments go in her own relationship. She stated she would see the choice her partner should make in a situation, and cringe when he did not take the right step. This would be hard for her because she could see the argument going poorly, know exactly why it was happening, and still feel very powerless to stop it.

Therapists are often expected to hold themselves to a higher standard in their relationships. During graduate school, I remember colleagues talking about their partners, saying things such as, "You're the therapist! How can you act like that if you are a therapist?" or "Don't you use those therapy skills on me!" In many ways, I think therapists can have a tougher time in their relationships because we have to walk a fine line between being ourselves and not trying to use therapy skills against our partners.

One of the things that can be helpful when your own relationship is in struggle is to do couples retreats or couples enrichment courses together. When couples get a chance to learn skills as a team, it can help our partners feel as though they have equal footing with us when it comes to conflict resolution and other relationship skills. Honestly, we do the same with the couples we work with. We have them learn skills as a team so they can improve together. As therapists, we also need to work together with our partners to improve our daily life.

I hope you understand that you are not a failure when you struggle in your own relationship. Marriage is hard, regardless of who is involved. Recently, *TIME Magazine* ran an article asking couples who have been married for many years (30+) to describe marriage (Luscombe, 2016). Each of the couples thought of their marriage as something they were very proud of, but at the same time they described marriage as either "hard" or "very hard!" It doesn't matter if you are a therapist who knows every relationship skill under the sun, or just a normal person making your way through life. Marriage is a tough road because we are trying to meet multiple needs and demands, while also managing a lot of stress and responsibilities. You are the best you can be! When you have a rough day, find a way to remind yourself that you are doing your best to be a good partner. If you are not being your best, then spend some time doing therapy of your own with your partner.

Milestone 6   Rebuilding Trust

Marcus and Tammy came into therapy after Marcus was found texting a co-worker. They had talked to each other for several weeks casually before Tammy found Marcus's text history. While the nature of the conversations had not turned sexual, the fact that he was keeping the relationship secret and was discussing details of their personal life jarred Tammy. She believed Marcus when he said the relationship was completely innocent, but she also struggled with feelings of betrayal that she couldn't quite name. Essentially, it felt as though a type of trust was broken between them.

In relationships, trust is something that is earned over time. When it comes to an affair, it can be difficult to move forward because it feels as though trust is completely destroyed. As clinicians, we can help couples by offering examples for how to build trust and then helping the couple identify specific action plans they will take to personally build trust.

As is the case with each of the milestones before this one, trust is not something that will magically go back to normal with a session or two. Clients need to understand that they will likely be earning trust for the rest of their relationship. That does not mean they will always be at square one when it comes to trust. It does mean that in various ways, the unfaithful partner and the hurt partner need to come to terms with how trust changes in the post affair relationship. It is a process over time that if done well can have long-lasting benefits.

Understanding Trust

There are several aspects to trust that a clinician needs to understand in order to help a couple rebuild trust with one another. First, there are many different realms in a relationship where a couple is capable of building trust. A few realms where trust is involved include financially, as co-parents, sexually, emotionally, in life goals, in careers, and in chores, to name a few. In each realm of a couple's life, they can either build trust or lose trust based on how they handle themselves within each of these realms. For example, when a couple creates a financial budget they both agree to, the more they each follow through with their financial goals, the more trust they build. However, in the same regard, if a budget is set for each partner to spend only $50 monthly, and each month a partner breaks that promise, over time trust is lost.

A betrayal of trust such as an affair can also affect these various areas. Depending on how big the betrayal, you will find your couples losing trust in the various realms while in other relationships, the breach in trust is solely related to their intimate relationship. We will go into this concept in more detail later in the chapter.

For starters, there are a few definitions/phrases that can be helpful for teaching trust to your clients. One phrase is called, "The benefit of the doubt." The Urban Dictionary explains this as, "to default to the belief that their intentions are honest, and not assume malice when there is uncertainty or doubt surrounding the circumstances" (Urban Dictionary Website, 2016). Usually in relationships, couples try to give each other the benefit of the doubt when they don't know the full story. However, after an infidelity, it may sometimes be difficult for the hurt partner to give the benefit of the doubt. They may often need a type of proof in addition to build trust.

Accountability is another term that will be helpful when teaching couples how to rebuild trust. Accountability is "the obligation of an individual or an organization to account for its activities, accept responsibility for them, and to disclose the results in a transparent manner" (Business Dictionary Website, n.d.). Part of what makes a person trustworthy is their ability to hold themselves accountable. For example, instead of expecting a partner to just trust your word, you instead show your word to be true. When you see clients say to their partner, "You should just trust me when I say I was at the party," you are not seeing someone who is trying to be accountable. To be accountable, they might say instead,

> I will be at this party from 6 to 8 pm. If at any time you want to join me, feel free. Or if you want to check in, I will be with my friend Jim. You have his number to call if you need to.

The second statement offers specific examples of how the person is trying to hold themselves accountable, while the first example is simply asking for blind trust. In accounting, the phrase they use commonly is "trust, but verify." Essentially, give people the benefit of the doubt, but check your facts.

A boundary is another term that is helpful in understanding trust. Merriam-Webster (2016) describes a boundary as, "unofficial rules about what should be done: limits that define acceptable behavior." I appreciate this definition because it is simplistic in nature and it points to the fact that a boundary is unofficial – meaning we are often unaware of where boundaries lie for the people around us. We each define acceptable behavior in different ways, based on how we were raised, our cultural and religious values, and specific incidents that we live through that shape how we view our world. A big part of rebuilding trust for clients will include setting clearer boundaries about what behaviors are acceptable and unacceptable going forward.

Privacy is another word that is important to explain to couples. The definition of privacy is varied in the dictionary. It includes freedom from damaging public scrutiny or secret surveillance; freedom from unauthorized disclosure of one's personal information; freedom from unwanted, undue intrusion; freedom to be left alone; solitude (Dictionary.com, n.d.). In many ways, it may feel unsafe for the hurt partner to offer privacy to the unfaithful partner because of how privacy has previously been used in the past against them. While I will cover this concept in more depth later in the chapter, it is important that both clients understand that parts of privacy may need to change for a time in order to rebuild trust. This does not mean the change will happen forever, but if there is no willingness to shift levels of privacy, you will see couples struggle to move forward.

A final point I use to describe trust is a math equation I came up with in a session. Over time, I have found this math equation to be a helpful way to break down trust in a very simple way.

$$\text{Earned Trust} = \frac{\text{Say} + \text{Do}}{\text{Time}}$$

To break this one down, trust is earned when a person does exactly what they say they will do over time. The more examples of situations where you do as you say you will do, the more that trust can be built. Essentially, when you say you will be at a hockey game and then show up at that hockey game, over time if you continue to show up at hockey games, your partner will trust that you will come to hockey games. The same is true of building trust with different realms in the relationship. If you say you will stick to a monthly budget of $100 and then you actually stick to it, over time I will trust you to stay within our budget. Essentially, trust needs to be redefined for your couples as something that can be earned or lost based on following through with mutually agreed upon behaviors.

Role of the Therapist

A challenging role you will play is helping couples to develop some perspective. Each partner, the hurt partner and the unfaithful partner, will have very unique views about trust that need to be shifted to a more reasonable place. However, your attempt to shift their viewpoint could prove very difficult.

A common statement I hear among the unfaithful partners is, "You'll never be able to trust me again," or "How can we move forward when she keeps bringing up the past?" Essentially, the unfaithful partner wants forgiveness and to know that the relationship could be rebuilt. They worry the relationship will be forever damaged. The challenge with this viewpoint is that in many ways the relationship is forever changed.

A reframe can help in this situation. I typically will say,

> I can see why you are worried. There are couples who work through affairs, but their relationships are never the same. That doesn't mean you can't improve your relationship or even have a better one than when you started. However, it will never be the same one you once had. You may need to come to terms with this fact.

This often makes them worry if they should even try. At this point, I try to suggest that many of the couples I have worked with have found ways to grow and mature as a couple in very deep and impressive ways. I remind them that improvement depends on their willingness to personally address the issues as a team.

You will find the hurt partner is also very extreme about how they look at trust. They will feel as though they could never trust their partner in the future. Again, you must offer some perspective.

> You may never give your partner the benefit of the doubt again, but that doesn't mean you won't be able to build trust. Trust is something that is built over time. You didn't start out fully trusting each other at the beginning of the relationship. In the same way, it will feel as though you are starting over in some ways.

It can be helpful to remind the hurt client about the beginnings of their relationship with their partner. Most people don't start out trusting a new relationship because it wouldn't be safe. They may give their new love the benefit of the doubt – meaning to assume this new partner is interested and wants to get to know them better. In reality, trust is something they build over time. The first time the new lover takes care of you when you are sick builds trust that they want to help you. The first time a new partner comes to your son's game, you begin to trust that they are invested in a future with you. Just like in the beginning of the relationship, trust will have to be rebuilt over time and with evidence that shows the unfaithful partner is invested in making the relationship strong again.

Interventions

There are a great number of interventions that I could list here. I will try to use the ones that have had the most impact for my practice. However, I encourage you as a clinician to look for other resources. There are many great books that discuss how to build trust. The four interventions I will discuss here include setting clear boundaries, trust is a two-way street, eradicating boundaries, and accountability.

Setting Clear Boundaries

When I cover boundaries with clients, I try to educate them on how best to use boundaries within their relationship. The most important thing clients need to understand is that they can never control another person. They can only control what they personally do. With that in mind, when clients set a boundary, the only way to control the outcome of the boundary is to take action on how they personally will respond to a behavior from their partner. Essentially, a boundary is first a request for an action or protection from someone else. Second, it is a plan for how you will respond to each outcome, i.e., if my partner follows through with this boundary I will respond this way; if my partner does not follow through with this boundary, I will respond this other way to protect myself. Either way, the boundary is set and is solely linked to the choices the requesting partner makes in response.

For example, Jane stated she set a boundary with James asking him not to use dirty talk during their sexual conversations. When Jane set that boundary, I asked her to make a plan for how she will react if he follows through and how she will act if he does not follow through. This is where real boundary setting takes place. After getting some help from me, she came up with an answer. She stated if he follows through with the boundary, she will develop more trust and feel more comfortable having sex with him. She hopes this will lead to more sex between them. If he does not follow through, she will likely need to have more conversations with him about why this boundary is important to her before she will feel comfortable having sex again. In either scenario, Jane is in control of the outcome. You can request that a boundary be set, but you cannot control the choice your partner makes as a result. The only way to actually set a boundary is by controlling your own behavioral choices.

To put it another way, companies set boundaries in business all the time. As clinicians, we often have a 24- or 48-hour cancellation policy. That is a boundary we request our clients to follow. However, we cannot control the choices our clients make. So, we also make a plan for how we will respond to a client complying or not complying with the boundary. If the client complies, we continue to see them in therapy and it's a non-issue. If the client does not comply, we either have a missed visit fee we charge or we have a set number of mistakes allowed before we might terminate therapy. In the same regard, the boundary has nothing to do with client compliance. A boundary is more associated with our personal follow through with keeping a boundary. Over time, we end up keeping clients who are more comfortable with our boundaries, and losing clients who are not comfortable with the boundaries.

Boundary setting is a very helpful way to help couples build trust both initially and long-term. However, some couples struggle with the idea of boundary setting. "I don't want to live in a relationship where I have to constantly check his every move," or, "I feel like boundaries won't control

the situation. If she wants to contact him, she will find a way to do it."
These are common responses from individuals who feel that boundaries
are a way of policing their partner or being policed by their partner. It also
feels like a losing game because, as I said before, there is no way to control
another person's behavior.

The best thing to do in this situation is agree with your client. It is not a
perfect system. It won't protect couples against every potential danger.
Also, it helps to remind them that boundaries usually start off more intense
in the beginning but then tend to relax over time. For example, Jane may
want Bill to always invite her to any outings he goes on with his friends for
the next six months. While it isn't reasonable to go to every outing with
Bill for the rest of their relationship, Jane may need Bill to put a lot of
initial effort in to show he is trying to be trustworthy. It can be helpful to
explain that boundaries will be more intense in the beginning, so that the
unfaithful partner doesn't lose hope in the relationship.

Going back to the original point, many times when your client is resist-
ant to a strategy, they really need to be heard and validated by you as a
clinician. The reality is that some of the boundaries may be difficult to
identify. While there are common ones, such as open access to emails and
phones or spending more initial time together, some boundaries are hard
to identify and don't necessarily fix the pain caused by the affair. I discourage you from putting too much weight on any intervention. These are
guidelines or ideas, but they don't replace your biggest job which is to
understand and respect your clients' needs in session.

Trust is a Two-Way Street

One of the biggest challenges I face when helping clients rebuild trust is
helping them to see how each of them plays a part in trust building. In the
initial phases of treatment, couples are often in high crisis. This time is
characterized by lots of fighting mixed with moments of truth, erotic
territory-marking sex, and various crazy making situations for both
parties. Once the initial crisis dies down, I start trying to help each of them
play a role in rebuilding trust.

James and Yolanda had made it through the first phase of therapy. They
were having fewer fights and were in general committed to working on
their relationship. However, Yolanda was struggling with being honest
about things to James. While she understood she needed to be honest to
rebuild trust, when she told him certain things he would over-react. This
made it harder for her to feel safe to tell him what was going on.

> It will be stupid things like how much money I spent or when I will get
> home. He has always been over-reactive to little things which initially
> made me start hiding things from him. Now that I am trying to be
> honest, I struggle with this reaction.

Couples need to understand that trust is a two-way street. Ideally, you want to help couples begin to have helpful conversations about boundary setting. However, if one person is very reactive, they will struggle to be honest about what is going on in their lives. In the case of Yolanda and James, I had to guide James in using a more neutral approach to get his needs met. While it makes sense for him to get angry if Yolanda lies, it also makes it harder for her to be truthful if she worries about his reaction all the time. If James can work on asking for his needs in a more neutral way, then Yolanda can start working on being more honest and trusting that James will try not to over-react.

I saw a similar case of this with Shawna and Grace. Prior to the affair Shawna had, Grace was a very reactive individual. Grace had been cheated on in a previous relationship. At the beginning of their relationship, Grace would get super jealous at times that often made no sense to Shawna. For example, Shawna and Grace worked together at the same company. Grace drove the forklift while Shawna worked on the floor. One day, Shawna was walking up to the front office in close proximity to another female co-worker. They weren't holding hands, they were in public, and nothing appeared to be happening from Shawna's perspective. However, when Grace drove past, she yelled loudly at Shawna and accused her of cheating with the other employee. The employee awkwardly backed away and let them talk, but the interaction did not end well. Shawna had many examples of being very jealous in awkward situations, which made Grace worry about what information she could be honest about. Over time, Grace would omit pieces of information that she worried Shawna would over-react about. This habit then made it easier to cheat on Shawna later in the relationship when the threat was real.

A big part of the trust building for Grace and Shawna, or the clients *you* may have, includes helping each partner take steps to be more honest and build trust. It's easier to be honest with a person who tries to hear your opinion and is neutral even when they disagree about things. Beyond this, it takes a partner who is willing to shift behaviors that feel uncomfortable to build trust.

Eradicating Threats

If the unfaithful partner continues in the affair, the threat has not ended. A big job you need to take on as the therapist is to help the couple eradicate any real threats left in the relationship. Part of this involves identifying the difference between a real threat and an imagined threat.

What is the difference? A real threat can be hard to detect. Essentially this involves looking at each client's vulnerabilities in their relationship or weak points. A weak point could be loose boundaries with parties of the opposite sex (or same sex if the client is bisexual or homosexual). A weak point could be when the unfaithful individual feels lonely or restless in their life. A weak point could be when they find someone attractive. Do they know how to let an attraction pass or do they think about it constantly? A weak point could be a tendency to get their needs met outside of the relationship rather than seeking help from their partner. Whatever the weak point, it is helpful to explore this idea in both individual and couple sessions.

One way to explore this idea is to help the unfaithful partner develop a better understanding of why they had the affair and what steps led them into the affair. A common story I hear is that the original couple either felt distant from each other for a while or recently had a fight. When they had the fight, instead of going to their partner about it, the unfaithful partner started commiserating with a co-worker they had a mild attraction to (at this point they have not cheated, but simply started a friendship). Next, they continue sharing secrets and helping each other out by listening, only to start being more flirtatious. At one point, one of them blurts out that they have feelings for the other person. At another point, the other person agrees they have feelings. Then, the relationship moves from an innocent friendship to romantic relationship.

When working with the unfaithful partner, it is important to hear and understand their story without bias to help them explore the reason why they did what they did. Over time, you have to help them explore both big and small choices they made, ways they justified their decisions, and lies they told themselves and their partner. When you develop a clear understanding, it makes it easier to identify specific vulnerabilities and helps your clients to put in safeguards to prevent these vulnerabilities from turning into an affair again. For example, if their weak point is getting drunk at bars, a safeguard might be to encourage them to only go to bars with their intimate partner or to avoid bars in general.

Redefining Privacy in Order to Be Accountable

Many couples struggle with how to rebuild trust because the actions required feel very invasive. Olympia and George were having this type of problem. When George cheated on Olympia, he often used "staying late at work" as an excuse. Now that he was committed to making the relationship work, he recognized that he needed to put the effort into being accountable for his actions. However, he still needed to go to work. While sometimes he used "late work nights" as an excuse, he still actually needed to work late some nights.

What needs to happen in cases like this is the couple has to find ways to be accountable to each other in more clear terms. They may need to be open to overdoing accountability in the beginning with the hope that this will eventually help their partner start to trust them again. An in the case of George, he offered that he would give Olympia access to his online work schedule so long as she would only look at it, and not do any tinkering. Olympia agreed to this because she didn't want him to lose his job.

However, some late nights are not listed in the schedule. For this situation, we had to get creative. I suggested an open phone call policy. At George's work, it's okay for a spouse to call his actual work number after hours because the job commonly keeps its employees late with little to no notice. Luckily, phone calls went through the receptionist first. So, if George was working late, Olympia was given permission to call his work number to check in and make sure he was actually working late and not actually going out with the other woman.

As a clinician, some of what you may need to do is get creative with clients about how to set up different types of accountability. It helps to let both clients know that this level of accountability may not be necessary for the long haul. It is a short-term fix to help them establish small amounts of trust right away. The hope is that, over time, less accountability will be required. But ultimately, I believe all couples should have some type of accountability to each other, regardless of past behaviors, to keep the relationship strong.

A Good Story

Sierra and Tony came into therapy after Sierra was found sexting with several other men on her phone. They were both around 40 and had lost some sense of connection to one another for a while. Tony stated he recognized that they had not been close for some time. The last few years, both of them got so focused on the kids that they felt a distance from one another. Sierra admitted she had used the sexting as a way to feel validated. She understood that it was a bad way to do things, but over the years, she had not felt Tony was willing to do anything to change their situation.

It was clear at the beginning of treatment that Tony and Sierra had already done a lot of talking to work on things. They reported to me they had gotten more honest recently than they had been in years. After some initial crisis reduction in therapy, it was clear that we needed to start building trust so they could move forward.

Sierra agreed to keep her phone out in a public place so that Tony could look at it any time. Tony also agreed that he would not check it constantly. Also, when he did check he would not yell at her if he found something suspicious. Instead, he stated he would work on asking her things neutrally without making assumptions. Sierra stated she would try to be upfront if there was anything he might be uncomfortable seeing in her phone.

Essentially, this couple was perfect for trust building because they both really wanted to make the situation better. During one session, I suggested they create a fidelity pact which comes from the book *After the Affair* by Janis Abrahms Spring (2012). A fidelity pact is an agreement a couple makes to let each other know right away if they have stepped outside the bounds of the relationship. Better yet, it is also an agreement to talk to each other if they are feeling close to stepping outside the bounds of the relationship. "Both partners are encouraged to articulate the types of situation, mood, and person that could draw them into an affair – and to share that information with each other" (Estroff Marano, 2012, p. 69).

This couple was very willing to work at this task. In fact, they spent several weeks discussing the various potential risks they each had at length. The most shocking part for me as a therapist was how mature Tony was working through things. He recognized that even though he did not cheat, he could have easily made a similar decision based on how their relationship evolved. Tony identified that when they focused solely on the children and not on each other, he found himself being flirtier with women at work and networking events. Sierra was a little more embarrassed to be outwardly flirty, but when men tried to connect with her on Facebook, that seemed like her challenge point. Sierra agreed to keep her phone available at any time and to let Tony know if someone tried to connect with her via Facebook. At the end of their therapy, they had been very honest and created a pact they both agreed could help prevent future mistakes.

A Bad Story

A common request I make of my clients is to tell their partner everything they can in the beginning about the affair. Essentially, the technique is similar to ripping a band-aid off. I tell the unfaithful partner that everything they tell their partner is going to hurt no matter what. It is better to let them know everything up front, hurt the hell out of them all at once, and then move on with trust building from there. I also try to explain that if they keep certain details secret, when these details come out later, it feels as though every bit of work they have done prior to that is ruined. It makes the couple feel like every bit of work done prior to the leak of new information didn't count.

After telling this to Dawn and Drew, they left the session feeling as though they at least had a plan for what to do next. They had agreed that they would talk every other day for 30 minutes, like I suggested, but then they would end the conversation and try to have fun. A week, several emails, and a wild number of confessions later, I had the couple back in my office. Apparently, Drew had not told the whole story up front. Under my advice, for the next week, he kept letting new and more difficult pieces of information surface.

First, Dawn found out that Drew actually had sex with the other woman (who continued to be called "the whore" in session). A day later, Dawn found out that he had been texting the whore for a while before they shared a drunken sex night. Two days later, Drew admitted to having gone to several strip clubs throughout their marriage. He also admitted to doing more than just paying for lap dances. Many of the clubs allowed you to engage in sexual liaisons with the strippers for a fee. Dawn found out that his affairs were chronic, his boundaries were often inappropriate, and he was struggling with constant thoughts about other women. By the end of the week, Drew confessed to feeling as though he was better than Dawn, smarter than her, and he was unsure if he was attracted to her.

At this point, I needed to have individual sessions to see just how far Drew's problem could go. He was having obsessive thoughts and questioning who he was as a sexual person. He also found that once he pulled the cord of honesty, it was like a flood of confessions he wanted to make, each one bigger and worse than the last, kind of like he didn't know how to stop himself.

In some of your cases, you may be dealing with people who struggle with compulsive sexual behaviors. As sex therapists, we do not use the term sex addiction because it does not show up in the DSM-V and it sometimes holds a religious connotation. However, we sex therapists absolutely see problematic sexual behavior and acting out. Some therapists label this additive personalities or sexual compulsivity. Other therapists choose terms like cybersex or sex addiction. Another group of therapists will label it sexual acting out in response to a DSM-V diagnosis such as borderline, bipolar, depression, etc. – meaning the acting out is a symptom of the mental health diagnosis.

However you choose to label the behavior, Drew clearly fits into a problematic sexual category. For clients who have only cheated with one person or for a short period of time in the grander scheme of the relationship, the tip to disclose early and as much as possible does help build trust. At first, it causes an extreme amount of pain and hatred, but over time, it makes it much easier for the hurt partner to move forward without fear that new information will come to light.

In the case of clients who have problematic sexual behavior, this same skill will have terrible effects and cause excruciating harm. In this case, I had to have several individuals with Drew. I spent some time trying to pin down a diagnosis, get him in individual treatment in addition to couples treatment, and get him to see a psychiatrist. When he was able to seek personal help, he was able to curb some of his obsessive thoughts and try to make better choices for his relationship. In the end, Dawn left Drew because she never felt she could trust him again.

Your Human Self

The more you work with couples affected by infidelity, the more you will find yourself struggling to trust things at times in your own relationship. It is common for me to hear a horrible story and then question the safety of my marriage. For example, one month my husband wanted to start a game night with the guys. I was okay with the idea so long as it went both ways, meaning the girls got a night and the guys got a night and we also put effort into a couple's night.

My husband had trouble with the added requirements. He stated he was just trying to create something with his friends. If we girls wanted something, that is fine, but he didn't know why the conversation was connected. He just wanted to make plans for his guys' night. I found myself very angry for a time about this, but couldn't put my finger on what the problem was. I just remember feeling overwhelmed when we had the conversations.

Over time and many conversations, we got to the bottom of things. Many of the stories I hear from couples dealing with affairs start in a similar way. After people have kids in their late twenties and their thirties, it gets harder to pay for babysitters or get family members to help watch the kids. Instead of date nights, couples will put time into guys' or girls' nights because the other spouse can be a babysitter. Over time, the couples put their relationship on the back burner. After some time, someone has an affair and they end up in my office devastated.

As I have said before, half of my practice involves helping couples overcome affairs. In my personal life, something very benign was becoming a serious issue, simply because it mimicked something I see in counseling every day. As clinicians, I urge you to recognize when you are getting counter-transference issues like this. The way I learned to recognize this is to notice when I am having a reaction to something that seems out of the ordinary. Hence my example, why would a guys' night be that big of a deal? When I notice myself feeling emotions that are too intense for the situation at hand, I look for potential counter-transference issues that could be at play. In this case, it took a while before I put the pieces together.

As always, I encourage you also to keep up with your self-care daily. When we see couples falling apart around us, it can take a toll on our lives. I encourage you to use these feelings as an opportunity to improve your own marriage. Start a date night or a shared hobby with your partner. As a result of this issue, my husband and I started a weekly painting session where we picked out a painting YouTube video to paint together at home. We also started something called dress up Sundays, in which we put on our best outfits to try and stay attractive to one another. These activities helped me feel like we made our relationship a priority.

Milestone 7   Redefining the Relationship

An infidelity has a way of making people really dissect their relationship. This can be a good thing if you, the clinician, can offer some guidance. Most relationships can improve in some way or another. Even if we look at our own relationships, we can probably point out several things we might want more of, including: more alone time with your partner, more time spent having fun together as a family, and less time focused on things that don't matter in the grand scheme of things, like the dishes or laundry!

I always encourage couples to make their relationship the best it can be. If couples use an infidelity as a catalyst for change, amazing things can happen going forward! This chapter is all about taking back the relationship in a way that makes the couple feel whole again.

Reframes are key at this stage of the game. A reframe is basically redefining a situation stressing the positive aspects (Nichols & Schwartz, 2006). Along the way in treatment, it can be helpful for the clinician to offer reframes that encourage the couple and help them to feel less broken.

I will reframe future situations by saying things such as, "You two have the chance to make a whole new relationship. While you can never have the old one back, the new one can be great! What do you want your relationship to look like?" I might say something else such as, "It is common for couples to reflect on life after an infidelity. What have you learned about yourself? What have you learned about your partner? What do you still need to be happy together?" Basically, you are trying to help them look forward to a more positive future.

When a couple starts getting to the point where they feel the situation has improved, you can talk to them about religious beliefs or personal values they hold that might help them start over. An example of this could be a renewal of vows or even a brand new proposal. They may choose some symbolic way to put the past behind them and look forward to the future, such as deleting those old emails or texts together. I had one couple go to confession together because this was symbolic of purging their sins and looking towards a more hopeful future.

In some cases, couples may want to discuss the nature of their relationship. While most couples in society are comfortable defining themselves as monogamous, I have had a few cases where couples wanted to discuss opening up their relationship in a more constructive way. I will cover how to have a productive conversation about this in detail later in this chapter.

As a sex positive therapist, I value all sexual styles so long as all partners involved find the situation mutually pleasurable. If both partners are expressing an interest in trying swinging, kink or a poly lifestyle, I am more than willing to have a frank conversation about this with clients. In fact, some people might say that polyamory is the antidote to infidelity because couples are allowed to have sex with multiple partners in a way that is more ethical than an infidelity. I am unsure if this is true or not. However, I have seen enough couples struggle with monogamy to wonder curiously about this lifestyle.

Is it more practical to be polyamorous? Are we as a society trying to live up to impossible ideals? Can anyone truly by monogamous? If your clients bring up this topic, I encourage you to help them have a neutral debate about the pros and cons of changing the nature of their relationship. If your clients do not bring this topic up, I would err on the side of caution with this topic. For some clients, the very mention of this topic brings up a lot of animosity.

During this phase of treatment, your role as a clinician is to be a neutral guide. Talk to your clients about what is out there. Explore ways other couples have used to redefine their relationship. Encourage clients to use whatever coping tools they already have on hand, such as religious or cultural values. Ultimately, find ways to help your couples develop resilience, which is the ability to utilize personal resources to recover from misfortune (Cherry, 2016). Another dramatic way to look at this concept is "a relationship reborn!" How do we help our couples get a fresh, new start on things?

Interventions

All of the interventions covered here are meant to help couples attempt to make a fresh start. Usually these are done after the initial crisis phase is over and after some work has been done to improve trust and improve the relationship.

Taking Back the Relationship

It is pretty common for my clients to struggle with specific dates regarding the affair. Maybe the affair lasted through the holidays. Maybe it happened around a birthday or anniversary. In many ways, these special dates have become tainted for the couple. The hurt partner will explain that they had noticed their partner was not invested around this time. In another scenario, even though the special day was a good day, the hurt partner has linked it with the timeline of the affair. Now they look back on these dates with confusion or bitter loss.

One of the interventions I offer couples later in therapy is to take back special dates in the marriage or relationship. I ask the couple to discuss any potential dates that seem sour as things are settling. Now that some time has passed, I encourage them to look forward to the upcoming special dates in the next years. I ask them the following questions:

> With [insert holiday or special date] coming up, you two have an opportunity to really make up for last year. How do you want to spend this day in a way that makes you feel loved and honored as a couple? Especially now that you two are heading on a better path!

I then guide the couple in a conversation about any important dates coming up. I encourage them to find ways to make these days special, even over the top.

Many of my couples find this helpful because they still struggle with the loss of their old relationship. Some part of them feels as though some memories have died or can never be the same. This exercise helps the couple make these dates even better than they were before. Rather than looking at these dates as potential reminders of the loss, it can be an opportunity to make their relationship better than it ever was before. Often, couples had gotten into a rut prior to the affair. They may have stopped getting presents for each other or even stopped doing romantic things for each other to celebrate the day. One of my favorite things about an affair is that it really jolts a couple into action. Many of them want a better relationship, they just need our help getting there.

There is an easy way to tell when a couple is ready to have this conversation. Look for the verb tense each person tends to use when talking about the infidelity. If your clients are still talking using either past tense or present tense, you know they are still going through things day by day. Actually, there are links to trauma and present tense speaking. When someone has recently been through a trauma, they often will state things like, "I am just taking things day by day." They won't be ready to talk about the future. Any attempt to guide them in the direction, they will avoid.

You can test this here and there by asking questions about any upcoming plans they have casually. Most couples will not be able to talk about anything beyond the next couple weeks or months right after the infidelity occurs. When they do finally start talking about a longer-term future with their partner, it is an indicator that they are moving out of the crisis phase and into a place where they are more willing to work on the future. At this time, you can begin to use this intervention to help them develop resilience as a couple.

Normalizing

Jane and Tiffany had been working through their affair for quite some time. They were experiencing more positive days with each other. However, every now and then they would experience a day or two that was not so great. Tiffany would feel down and start to remember the betrayal. She would try to talk to Jane about it. Jane would try to talk her through things but after a certain point she would stop the conversation. Throughout it all, a common conversation they had in session afterwards sounded like this, "I wish you could acknowledge that we are having some good days and improving." This comment would be followed by this comment, "It feels like Jane wants me to just get over things quickly. I am still working through some of these issues."

When a couple has this discussion, I try to normalize the situation. I state that it is common for couples to struggle with this conversation. Neither person is right or wrong. Instead of fighting over whether you are having good or bad days, both of you need to work on acknowledging the good days when you have them and acknowledging the rough ones as well. Having a bad day does not erase all the good days that have happened. Having several good days also does not erase the bad that happened.

Essentially, I try to help each person move away from their extreme positions and give each other credit. Another helpful thing is to encourage couples to enjoy good days when they have them, and work through bad days when they have them. Couples have to accept both parts of this process in order to truly heal. This is similar to mindfulness. Essentially, you are trying to help the couple deal with the here and now. Neither partner needs to push the other to move forward too quickly. In anything worth fighting for, these things take work and time to heal. Try your best as a clinician to normalize their struggle so they can effectively move through things as a team.

Here is an example conversation that I coach couples to use for the different kinds of days. For a bad day:

PERSON 1: I'm sorry today was a rough/bad day.
PERSON 2: Me too. I am sorry we had a bad day. Let's try and make tomorrow a better day.

For a good day:

PERSON 1: I think we had a good day. Was it good for you?
PERSON 2: It was a good day. I am thankful for the day we had today. Let's try it again tomorrow.

The important part of these conversations is that no matter who starts the conversation, the second person is acknowledging the first person. If it is a good day, acknowledge and appreciate the good day. If it is a bad day, acknowledge and respect the struggle as a couple. As clinicians, we cannot predict whether a day will be good or bad. Neither can our clients. This type of conversation at least helps them each feel acknowledged.

Discussing Polyamory

A recent discussion that has become very common in my practice after an affair is a discussion about opening up the relationship. Currently, around 4–5 percent of the population has admitted to being openly in a polyamorous relationship (Khazan, 2014). In addition, a large number of people have at least considered this lifestyle or talked about it in their relationships.

There are some real challenges to facing this question after an affair. People who proclaim polyamory as a life choice believe that it is important for all adults to consent to the choices made sexually. There should be no sexual partner who is not aware of the life they are trying to lead. In an affair, all parties did not consent to the sexual or relationship act. The only consenting parties are the two people who had the affair. Usually the partners find out after the betrayal.

My first order of business when this topic is brought up is to guide the couple towards working through their issues first. Polyamory can complicate the healing process. It has been my experience that when couples attempt polyamory to try and fix a broken relationship, it distances them even further. I encourage the couple to work on building their relationship foundation. If after they have healed some, they want to consider this lifestyle, they can consider it a few months or even a year down the road.

When couples do decide to consider polyamory, there are a few resources you can guide them to use to explore this concept. One book is called *The Ethical Slut,* by Easton and Hardy. This book covers a variety of open relationship styles and tries to offer an ethical standard by which the couple can consider the consequences of the choice to open a relationship. One final resource you can use is Poly Role Models which can be found at www.facebook.com/polyrolemodels/. This Facebook page draws stories from actual people living a polyamorous lifestyle. They share their stories, their failures, and the lessons they have learned along the way.

Another book that is more of a fiction that couples can read is called *The Harrad Experiment* (Rimmer, 1990). In this book, the author provides an interpretation of polyamory in a type of utopian society in which the couples are very mature and capable of having an open relationship in a positive way. For couples who really don't know what a poly relationship would look like, I think this book tries to offer a glimpse into the positive aspects of this lifestyle.

Finally, I would encourage you to teach your couples a model for sexual ethics that comes from Douglas Braun-Harvey and Michael Vigorito (2016). This model is very basic and really crosses many sexual cultures. For sex to be ethical, these are the core requirements for each individual:

1   Sex is consensual for all parties.
2   Sex is non-exploitative (all parties are capable of consenting).
3   Partners are honest with each other about needs/desires.
4   Sex is mutually pleasurable.
5   Couples have shared values.
6   All parties are protected against STIs/unwanted pregnancies.

At least with a set of ethical guidelines, your couples can very clearly know if a choice they make is acceptable or unacceptable. Beyond a basic code of ethics, they still may need some therapeutic guidance.

A Good Story

Jill and David had been coming to therapy for about six months. Jill cheated on David long ago during a girls' night out. She had too much to drink and kissed a stranger on the dance floor. Right away she felt terrible and told her husband. They came into therapy afterwards to work through the trust issue because they knew they could not do it alone.

They had done a lot of good work up until this point. Jill had found great ways to take ownership and had recommitted to the relationship. David had even changed a lot about himself to improve the relationship. He realized they had gotten into a rut in their relationship and, essentially, they both had grown bored with one another. While he was not happy with what Jill did on the dance floor that night, he had started to see it as a symptom of a bigger problem in the relationship.

Now that they had worked through a lot of the initial issues, a new problem emerged. They would have a week or two pass that was really positive in which they both worked at things and saw great improvement. However, there were still these days randomly that seemed to throw them for a loop. One of them would feel bad and bring the other one down. They both would read each other's moods and not know what caused it or what to do about it.

I asked them if there were any important dates or cultural references to affairs that tended to happen around the days they felt bad. Jill pointed out that if they watched a show that referenced an affair, they seemed to be fine watching it, but then the next day would be rough as though they were being triggered. David started recognizing this as well, only his were more linked to when she mentioned hanging out with those same friends again. Even though they weren't the reason she cheated, David was very hurt that it happened while some of her friends were nearby. No one had stopped the situation.

I encouraged them to address these feelings directly. It is very common for couples to have triggers that create a painful emotion. These triggers can come from cultural references, passing by locations where the affair took place, and dates that connected to the original event such as birthdays or anniversaries that might have been tainted. I let them know that it is very commonplace for couples to still have triggers for a while after an affair. The best thing to do was talk to each other, share they are struggling that day, and find ways to support each other through that struggle. I explained that I can't stop bad days from occurring, but they could at least feel loved and supported when these things happened.

From that point on, David and Jill talked to each other when it got rough. If a show came on that referenced an infidelity, either one would stop the show and ask their partner, "Is it okay for us to watch this, or do we need to turn this off?" This helped them have an honest discussion and decide either consciously to avoid the show or to watch it knowing that they were going to be okay.

As for the friends, Jill asked him how he felt about her hanging out with her friends before making plans. She would ask if he needed her to do anything during the night to reassure him or even if he wanted to come. David appreciated this and usually did not need anything more than a text saying she loved him at some point. Her willingness to consider his feelings with these outings helped him to trust she had good intentions around the evenings out. Over time, David was able to trust her going out again without having the same trigger response.

A Bad Story

It is common for me to use the intervention of "Taking Back the Relationship." Specifically, I suggest you bring this up with clients after they have gotten through some of the major hurdles in treatment. Recently, I had a couple, Joanna and Zach, who had been with me in therapy for about six months. They were at the point in therapy where they started to come monthly for checkups and to talk through any lingering challenges around the infidelity.

I asked Joanna if there were any important dates coming up that reminded her of this time. Joanna thought back to the timeline when she first learned about the affair and the dates that happened prior to "D-Day" as they referred to it. Joanna explained that Valentine's Day was when she found out about Zach's affair.

I explained the importance of taking back these special dates in a proactive way. Many of my couples find some value in reinventing these days in a way that makes them feel special and really takes care of the relationship. Some couples may rewrite their vows. Other couples will re-create their first date on Valentine's Day or their anniversary, to symbolize the way they have grown as a couple.

Joanna started to cry at this point. She stated that lately she had been looking back over pictures of her baby shower and when her daughter was born with sadness. The affair started around the time of her baby shower and lasted until after their daughter Belinda was born. This was their only child. She was angry that he had cheated at this time. Now, something that was meant to be beautiful and special was laced with a bitter memory. As Joanna put it, "I cannot relive her birth or my pregnancy. There is no easy way to recreate or celebrate these memories."

I watched Zach's expressions. He was both confused and guilty. "I thought you had gotten over some of these feelings," he stated. She shook her head and explained she just didn't talk about her sad feelings anymore. "What's the point of bringing up the painful memories?" she replied. I realized that an event like this could not easily be replicated or taken back.

Instead of going in that original direction, I suggested they find ways to remain close on the anniversaries of these dates. I explained that she should let him know what dates from the previous year were the most painful. I encouraged Zach to intentionally do things to be close with her and a little kinder to her on these dates. In this way, they could at least come together rather than distance from one another. I also suggested they still find ways to do something nice for each other during these dates. Joanna stated actions seem to help her out more than words. She asked him to contact her a lot through the day and spend the evening alone with their daughter doing something fun. He promised to do so.

Not every story has an easy ending. I wished I could find a way to re-create that birth so that she did not have to associate such a beautiful event with such a painful memory. I think Zach wished the same. The reality is that life is not always perfect. Sometimes, we just have to offer our best advice given a painful situation. Staying close and kind to one another is better than nothing.

Your Human Self

The number of people affected by infidelity is staggering. Whether you are in a relationship that has been affected by an affair or someone close to you has been affected by this issue, it is likely that you have some values and beliefs about this topic. One of the challenges we have as clinicians is that our job is to attempt to be objective and help our clients in the best possible way. How do we stay objective with a topic that comes loaded with judgment and social criticism?

I am going to introduce you to a useful exercise centered around personal counter-transference. Please understand that the following is a potential triggering exercise. Proceed with caution. Here are a few questions you may ask yourself to find out a little more about how your values affect your decisions in therapy:

1   What are your personal values about marriage?
2   What are your personal values about infidelity including: What to do? What not to do? Who should be informed? How should information be shared within the family, etc.?

3   Have you or anyone in your close personal circle been affected by infidelity? How did it affect you? How did you react? How do you feel about the way you reacted?
4   Have you come to terms with this experience or do you still hold onto unresolved feelings about this?
5   How do you think these experiences affect the way you work with clients going through infidelity?
6   If you see yourself struggling with counter-transference around this issue, what are some of the ways that you can seek support?

I want to make sure every clinician understands that I don't do this exercise to make you feel blamed, criticized, or incapable of doing this work.

I was trained that counter-transference is a normal part of therapy. In my training, no one suggested that struggling with an issue means you cannot help people struggling through those same issues. However, when you don't recognize your struggle and work through it, then there can be ways that you react in therapy that are not productive for your clients. There are many ways to work through counter-transference. First, seek helpful supervision from a group or a specific adviser. We all need a fresh perspective from time to time. Second, find ways to regularly check in with yourself on how you are reacting in sessions. Are you staying calm? Are you able to maintain relative neutrality for each client? Finally, seek your own therapy if you need it. Therapy has helped me through many walks of my life. If you are still struggling with feelings from the aftermath of an infidelity, it's okay to admit you need more support and it will help you be a better clinician in the long run.

Milestone 8　Reclaiming a Healthy Sex Life

One of the biggest challenges for a couple post affair is helping them to improve their sex life. In many ways, the hurt partner struggles with how to be sexual again with their partner. An affair feels like the deepest betrayal. Depending on if the affair turned out to be sexual, ideas or images of the potential affair can haunt the hurt partner when they try to reintroduce sex into their relationship.

After an infidelity, the hurt partner has to decide how to proceed. They find themselves stuck between wanting to do everything they can to keep their partner and wanting to get as far away as possible. The types of sex that couples engage in post affairs include competitive sex, angry sex, avoidance of sex, and using sex to try and win each other back or build trust. While some version of this experience is completely normal given the situation, it can be hard for clinicians to guide clients toward how to resume their sex life with their partner.

My first goal is to make sure a couple is ready to address sex in therapy. If you move too fast with clients in this area, you will naturally hit road-blocks. I tell couples up front that we will cover sexuality in their sessions at some point. Then, I reassure them that sex will not be addressed until they feel comfortable talking about it. During each session, I do make references to sex in a casual way. I do this because the more you make the subject of sex a comfortable topic, the easier it is for the couple to bring up the subject. If you never approach sex at all, the couple may assume it is not okay to talk about sex with you. Casual information here and there helps them develop comfort with the topic.

When couples do start broaching the conversation of sex, I am very respectful and supportive of their experience. Some couples are already having sex but struggling with PTSD symptoms. In their study on emotional reactions to cheating, Schneider et al. (2012) suggest that a romantic betrayal by a long-term partner can create symptoms in the hurt partner that are consistent with a trauma response. The symptoms tend to be long-lasting. Naturally, some of these symptoms are going to occur in their sex life. As a clinician, it is helpful to use trauma informed care practices when treating clients and their sex lives.

One way to explain traumatic symptoms includes defining the symptoms as triggers. A trigger is a symptomatic reaction from one of the five senses that directly relates to the traumatic event (DerSarkissian, n.d.). When the infidelity took place, different senses become associated with the event that can then become triggers later on in life and in their sex life. These act like buttons that turn on your body's alarm system (DerSarkissian, n.d.).

People behave in different ways as a result of these triggers. Some people try to avoid thinking about the triggers. Some people will force themselves to push through a sexual experience and hope that the triggers will eventually go away. Other people will need to stop having sex in that moment and either talk or take alone time. Yet others will set boundaries around their sex life for a time until they feel more in control of the triggers.

My focus here is to encourage partners not to pressure each other into having sex before they both are ready to do so. In some cases, if the way they are having sex seems to be causing harm, I will at least offer some suggestions for how to make their sex life a little better for the time being. It is perfectly fine for the couple to improve their sex life over time rather than trying to go 100 miles a minute to improve everything all at once.

Learning to Talk About Sex

If you can't get a couple to talk about sex, it is going to be hard to help them have good sex. One of the first lessons I teach all my couples is to change the way they talk about sex. Many couples are either using a fighting/critical style of communication about sex or they are avoiding the conversation altogether. Neither of these sexual styles helps them have better sex. When there is infidelity, these conversational styles can be exacerbated as a result of the betrayal.

I encourage couples to start using a different communication style around sex. One communication style is non-judgmental, curious conversations about sex. When couples talk in this intellectual way, I am asking them to be somewhat clinical. Their job is to be curious, to explore nonjudgmentally, and to learn about various aspects of sex they have not been educated about before. They are to avoid putting any pressure on their partner but to develop a healthy curiosity about their partner's sexual world or lack thereof. The sexual history questionnaire which is a hallmark of sex therapy assessments offers some very helpful open-ended questions couples can begin to ask each other. The only goal of intellectual conversation is to understand each other better and to understand the fundamentals of sex better.

The second style of communication I teach couples to use is a playful/fun or even flirtatious style. Many times, this is the way that couples begin to flirt or enjoy sexual conversation. If you can play and have fun when you talk about sex, then you can start to play and have fun in your actual sexual experience. You still have to take a very non-judgmental listening role during this type of conversation. In order to help couples understand this conversational style, I will often explore different ways that couples flirt. This may include jokes, competitiveness with good sportsmanship, compliments, goofy teasing, and encouragement.

One very important aspect for either conversational style is to avoid any type of criticism. In their book about what makes marriage work, Gottman and Silver (2015) describe criticism as a global or absolute problem with the partner. This may show up in a sexual conversation in the following way, "You never want to try anything new," or "You just aren't a very sexual person." Both of these statements are criticisms because they are stating something globally about the partner's relationship with sex. Criticism has a natural way of de-motivating your partner. Instead of wanting to have sex with you, your partner is likely to feel defeated and feel like a failure. There are many ways that couples have essentially criticized each other out of even liking their sexual experiences.

That doesn't mean a partner can't talk about sex or their sexual interests. It just means the framing needs to be more intellectual or playful. An intellectual way to show an interest in sex may include, "I have recently been seeing stories about sex toys. Have you ever tried one? Do you know anything about sex toys? Do you have any values for or against sex toys?" The previous questions are very open ended and matter of fact. The person is exploring the topic of sex toys in a neutral way. There is no suggestion that the partner has to use a sex toy. There is just a curious conversation to learn more.

If a person is approaching the same topic being playful, they may say to their partner, "I would love to try a sex toy one day. What do you think?" and it might progress to something like, "It might be interesting to just buy one so we could have a sword fight with them." It's playful, silly, but it's still stating an interest in trying something and gauging how well a partner reacts. If the partner is open to playing, they might shoot back, "Well if we go to one of those stores, maybe we should play with them there to see if they meet our sword requirements!" I try to model both types of conversation in session so couples can get comfortable talking amongst themselves. I also explain both styles and ask them to pick one style to start, whichever is most comfortable for them. It's okay to start with one conversational style and move into the other.

There are so many different ways that couples can begin to work on their sex life that I cannot cover every one of them in the scope of this book. To learn more as a clinician, I encourage you to read any of the following books: *Come as You Are*, by Emily Nagoski; *Mating in Captivity*, by Esther Perel; *The Guide to Getting It On*, by Paul Joannides; *Becoming Cliterate*, by Laurie Mintz.

Ideally, I would like to see clinicians helping clients in the following areas when it comes to sexual health and development: learning to communicate comfortably about sex; exploring their personal interests sexually; sharing their personal interests with one another; understanding differences between male and female desire; building trust; learning to be vulnerable; and learning how to consent to various sexual acts, including basic affectionate touch. There are many more sexual topics that could be beneficial to couples. Make sure you learn as much as you can to personalize treatment to fit your clients' needs.

There are some couples therapists who do not cover sexual issues in affair treatment. I feel this is a disservice to some clients. I have many clients who went to therapy treatment for an infidelity but then came to me as a sex therapist because they still felt their sex life was struggling. Sometimes affairs happen as a result of people being unhappy in their sex life. Other times a couple's sex life takes a hit because they have lost trust after the affair. Either way, your couples need to feel safe enough to address their challenges with you so they can fully heal.

Role of the Therapist

As a clinician, it is very important to assess to what degree the affair has affected a couple's sex life. Here are a few examples of questions you may ask to learn more:

1   What was your sex life like before the affair took place?
2   What is your sex life like now? Are you still having sex? Why or why not?
3   Were there any struggles sexually you have had in your relationship in general? Did you ever try to resolve these? Were you successful?
4   How has this affair affected your ability to enjoy sex with your partner?

These are only examples of a few questions, but they can open up a substantial amount of information. Part of what you need to find out is to what degree sex is a part of why the affair took place for the unfaithful partner. The more I ask these questions of my clients, the more I find out that unhappiness sexually was one contributing factor to why some partners become unfaithful. (Not all couples have this same issue.)

I want to be very clear here. It is never the right choice to have an affair. I truly believe that an affair hurts people very deeply on both sides. An affair shakes the core of the person who stepped outside of the marriage. At the same time, an affair causes the hurt partner to question almost every aspect of the marriage. Rather than cheating, I would hope to help every one of my clients have a happy healthy sex life! I wish instead of this occurring, couples could be honest with each other about their unhappiness and find a way to get help. However, like most of you already know, it is more common to see a couple after an affair has taken place. The average couple waits seven years after problems start before coming in to seek help. While the ideal situation would involve a couple making a conscious choice to work through their problems without making the situation worse, the reality is we clinicians often have to work through sexual problems after a person has cheated and caused what feels like irreparable damage.

With that being said, if there are sexual problems in the relationship, a couple has not completely healed until you have addressed any sexual issues that are unresolved. Just having the willingness to ask questions and assess for areas sexually that could be problematic could help couples begin to improve the situation.

Your role as a therapist is to avoid assigning blame while also assessing for ways the couple's sex life can improve. If a couple's sex life was bad prior to an affair, you may also need to assess what kind of sexual relationship each partner wants currently. One of my most common questions in the beginning of treatment for the hurt partner is, "When is it okay for me to have sex again with my partner?" The answer to this question is very personal. I usually answer by offering different stories about how other clients in their position decided they were ready for sex again. Ultimately, a couple should have sex when they both feel ready to do so and not a second sooner.

Interventions

The following interventions offer some options on how you can address sexuality with couples in a more direct way. Each intervention is meant to help couples get comfortable talking about sex, learning about their personal interests and desires, and being more direct about their sexual needs with their partners.

Good Enough Sex Model

Gina and Ricky were a young couple. Ricky had a one-month affair with a co-worker that started while Gina was in her final stages of pregnancy. Gina found out about the affair two months after it happened when she received a secret phone call giving her the details of one of Ricky's encounters. When Gina confronted Ricky, his guilt showed clearly on his face and he admitted to making a mistake. The next week, they showed up in my office.

Upon further assessment, I found out that Ricky had been very unhappy with their sex life for about three years. He had tried to initiate sex more or to be romantic, but nothing seemed to help the situation with Gina. As one part of their treatment, I worked on the Good Enough Sex Model with this couple (Metz & McCarthy, 2007).

The Good Enough Sex Model has 12 principles for a healthy sex life. One of my most common interventions is to go through each principle one by one in therapy. I frame this intervention by stating,

Most couples only learn the problematic parts of sex or what things you can do wrong. This model tries to give couples ideas for how to have a healthy sex life. I will read each principle one by one and ask you to offer your opinions, beliefs, and values about the principle. I am not looking for an agree/disagree statement. I am more interested in learning what it makes you think about – the memories it brings up, the values it may challenge.

In each session, we cover anywhere from one to five principles in depth.

The key to this intervention is not to just send them the article to quickly read and never address again. By reading it through slowly in sessions, I am able to assess for lack of education around sex, lack of desire, understanding about each other's sexual values, and a variety of missing pieces that could contribute to a healthier sex life.

While discussing this model with Gina and Ricky, the first principle* stirred up a lot of discussion: "Eroticism is an intentional feature and the responsibility of each partner" (Metz & McCarthy, 2012, p. 216). First, the couple asked me to describe eroticism to them. My most simple answer for this is,

> What is erotic is what is hot or sexy to you. You can be having sex that is not erotic – more bland or boring. You can not be having sex at all, but see a glimpse of the bra of a woman as she bends over to tie her shoes, and find this erotic. Eroticism is something you personally find sexy and erotic.

After hearing the explanation, they both agreed they had never really been intentional about their eroticism. Sometimes the mood would strike them and they would have sex. Other times, many weeks could pass before something erotic stirred the pot between them. They had also never thought about eroticism being a responsibility. I pointed out that it is very common for couples to wait for a feeling of desire to engage sexually with one another. However, this habit is one reason why a couple sometimes drifts into a sexless marriage. Couples who have healthy sex lives realize that it takes some work to keep that spark going. Day-to-day, they do things to entice and attract each other – flirting, kissing, cuddling, innuendo, playfulness, etc. I find a great deal of value in teaching all of these principles to my clients because too many couples have had little to no sex education throughout their lives. This is a shame.

I would be careful about the timing of this intervention or any sex intervention. I always offer this model as an option, but I let my couples decide when they are ready to talk about sex. It can be common for a couple to avoid sex for a time after infidelity occurs. It can be just as common for a couple to have sex right away after an infidelity. Either way, check in and make sure your clients are open to the feedback.

The No Pressure System

A big challenge most of the couples I work with are going through is that sex has become pressured. Even when there is no affair present, I am hearing the same comments from my couples as their sex life is starting to decline. Jimmy and Tina are a perfect example of this. When we started to explore their sex life, it had been a good three years of rare sex at best. Jimmy always desired sex and would try to initiate. However, Tina always felt pressured by him and would shut down sexually. She did not feel desire for sex at all. Over time this caused a rift in which they would go for weeks and at times months without sex until Jimmy finally brought it up in frustration. By that time, Tina felt she did not want to have sex with him because they were arguing about it. Nothing was done to try and resolve this. Eventually Jimmy stopped trying and gave up on his sex life. It was around this time that he met Rhonda who he eventually had an affair with.

After doing some work to help Jimmy and Tina build trust, we had to start discussing how sex had become pressured. Essentially, Tina stopped feeling any desire for sex at all. When she first noticed this, she hoped it would eventually go back to normal. She waited and tried to avoid sex with Jimmy in the meantime. As time passed, she focused on other activities. Life became busy with their two children and she was easily able to avoid his advances at times when they were tired. One thing she did was avoid affection or any flirting with her partner. She began to feel bad as though she would be leading him on if she tried to show any affection. This created more of a distance and actually caused her desire to plummet even further.

After talking for some time about it, Tina stated she wanted to find her desire again. She knew that it was a problem but never knew what to do to fix the situation. At this time, I suggested they work as a couple on creating a "no pressure" system. This basically means that I teach a couple how to enjoy every intimate act for the act alone. This is a version of mindfulness. Linehan (2014) describes mindfulness as being fully present and in the moment. A sexual mindfulness is needed to experience more positive sexual energy as a couple.

What I teach couples to do is to kiss mindfully: to be fully present in the moment of kissing and not to try and move things to the next step; to enjoy kissing for the sake of kissing. One of the reasons people struggle sexually is that they feel pressured to advance to the next level before they are ready to do so. As a result, they shut their own desire down by avoiding the positive feelings associated with the current action. For example, Tina would either avoid kissing, or if she did kiss, her mind would be elsewhere. She would worry about whether she was sending the wrong message to her partner. In the "no pressure" system, I have couples practice simply kissing because kissing itself is fun. I try to encourage them to make it clear to their partner verbally that it is okay to just kiss at this moment and nothing else.

I do this with a variety of sexual activities such as massage, making out, flirting, watching sexual content on television, etc. This is a form of responsive desire. Responsive desire is desire in response to internal or external cues in the environment (Leiblum, 2007). These cues could include watching sexy images, reading a sexy book, wearing a sexy outfit, flirting, thinking about sexy things, kissing, etc. When women or men are given the opportunity to engage in sexual cues without pressure from their partner, it makes it easier for them to explore what actually turns them on sexually. No matter who you are, you need to feel free to be a sexual person before you can share sexuality with a partner comfortably.

In couples where there is pressure to perform, over time women or men (depending on who receives the pressure) tend to shut down. By creating a system in which they engage sexually in fun and playful ways with no pressure, over time they start to feel more sexually connected and want to have sex more. The key is for the lower desire person to be mindful and focus on their sensations – touch, vision, sounds, tastes, and smells. I help them to focus their attention on the erotic sensations that happen while they kiss, cuddle or share a massage.

Beyond mindful intimacy or engaging in cues, as a therapist you can look for ways a partner puts pressure on things. The man may yell at his wife if she refuses too frequently to have sex. The woman may pressure her husband by saying, "Every other man initiates with his wife. What's wrong with you?" Essentially, pressure shuts down the other partner. As clinicians, we need to offer more respectful ways to ask for sexual needs. For example, "I would love it if we could make out tonight," or "Is there anything I can do to help you relax and maybe get sexy together?" One way I have been redefining the initiation is to suggest that couples initiate "intimacy of some sort." Maybe they consent to cuddling naked and massaging each other. It is fine if things stay there, but if they both start feeling more sexual in response to the massage, they make the decision together to move forward.

Trigger Response Treatments

When infidelity is associated with sex, often the hurt partner can become triggered during their sexual episodes. For example, James and Monica had come into therapy to work on their sex life post affair. They had already spent time working through trust issues and rebuilding their relationship with another therapist. However, their sex life continued to suffer. James, the hurt partner, reported that he could not get images of his wife having sex with another man out of his head. Many times, they would be intimate. However, he would find himself thinking about different sexual activities or positions, and worry that he wasn't as good sexually as the other man was. This would take him out of the moment and cause some erectile difficulty.

Affairs affect individuals by causing PTSD-like symptoms. "The betrayed partner may experience depression, rage, feelings of abandonment, a sense of rejection, lowered self-esteem, loss of confidence and symptoms of post-traumatic stress disorder" (Fife et al., 2013, p. 344). In the case of James, he essentially was having PTSD triggers during sex or flashbacks to the events.

One helpful treatment for addressing triggers is to help the clients work through and process their triggers. Wendy Maltz (2012) discusses a four-step process in which clients can do the following:

1   Stop – observe a trigger is happening and stop what you are doing.
2   Calm – do something to physically deescalate such as deep breathing or self massage.
3   Affirm reality – do something to emotionally deescalate such as remind yourself where you are, that you are in control, and nothing has to happen right away.
4   Alter activity – either do something different or continue doing the same thing but feeling more in control and empowered.

To break this down further, both the individual on their own and with their partner can use this process to begin to heal their sex life as a team.

Individually, James was instructed to notice when he would get triggered by thoughts day-to-day or even while having sex. Once he observed it was happening, he was then instructed to do something to calm himself down physically such as taking deep breaths, rubbing his hands together, or noticing his body in space and time. For example, he could notice his back against a chair, the sounds of the room, or whether he was sitting straight or slouched.

After doing something to physically calm down, he was instructed to mentally calm down and affirm his reality. He could say to himself, "I am here because I want to be here. I don't have to do anything I don't want to do. I am in a room. I am on a bed. I am with my wife. I am home." Clients are instructed to repeat steps 2 and 3 as often as they need to in order to calm down and feel safe again. Then, once they feel more relaxed, they can either continue to do their current activity with a clear conscious head, or choose to do something different.

Couples can use this same process during sex to alter the trigger response. For example, if James were to have a trigger during sex, he would try to observe the trigger then ask his wife, "Can we stop for a moment? I am having some painful memories." His wife can then understand he is having a trigger and try to offer assistance. They can deep breathe together. It is helpful to have the couple discuss what they will do to calm down one another as a team. In this case Monica was instructed to sit next to James with her hand on his knee while he did things to physically and emotionally calm down.

If James struggled, he could ask her to say some calming things such as, "We are here together. It's okay for us to sit and relax. I love you. Nothing is happening right now." Many of my couples have found it helpful to identify reassuring comments that can be said by their partner ahead of time because it can be difficult in the moment to come up with the words to say. James reported it was helpful to hear Monica say calming things because sometimes he gets so lost in his own head that he struggled to come up with reassuring thoughts on his own. He liked that Monica offered an external monologue that he could listen to. In some ways, he felt hypnotized by the tone and soothing nature of her words.

After going through the steps as a team, Monica and James would have a conversation about what to do next. Did they want to continue making love or did they need to cuddle and talk for a while to get back into the mood? This trigger intervention has been very helpful for couples like Monica and James. Often, prior to the triggers, both partners would have times where they just weren't fully present sexually with one another. This process offered a very specific approach for how they each could bring that out in the open and be supportive to each other, rather than trying to push through the sexual experience and deal with things. I would encourage clinicians to use this process often with couples, regardless of whether or not they are going through the triggers of an affair.

Talking About Sexual Needs and Desires

Many couples have not had a lot of education about what normal desire looks like and how it can be different for men versus women. In every one of my books, I try to devote one chapter to educating clinicians and clients about what healthy sex looks like for happy couples.

There are two types of sexual desire clinicians need to know about, responsive desire and spontaneous desire (Lieblum, 2007). Spontaneous desire is the kind most linked to the natural hormonal urges people experience day-to-day. During the teenage years, most people will report higher spontaneous desire levels. The boys in middle school often could tell stories of getting an erection in the middle of class and then getting called to write some example from the homework on the board. Those erections or natural hormones that create desire tend to be higher in adolescence and shift over time based on each individual's biological makeup.

The second type of desire – responsive desire – refers to experiencing desire in response to specific cues that can be internal or external. For example, a person may think about an old sexual experience they had with a partner that was super sexy. In response to thinking intently about this experience, they may become aroused by this internal cue. Another example, a woman may not be in the mood initially, but she may respond to her partner as they engage in affectionate petting while watching a TV show together. This is desire in response to an external cue.

Every individual is very different when it comes to desire. Commonly, women will state they tend to experience desire more in the form of responsive desire, while men will state they tend to experience more of the spontaneous desire. However, men and women can differ. There are plenty of women who state they experience spontaneous desire. There are plenty of men who state they only experience responsive desire. The important piece here is that we educate couples about what is common when it comes to desire so couples don't argue about differences that are normal sexually.

In her book *Come as You Are* (2015), Nagoski discusses that sexual desire can be likened to driving a car. There are some people who are often on the "go" pedal. At any given time, if sex is a possibility, they are going to go for it, despite what may be happening day-to-day. There are other people who are more context dependent when it comes to their desire. Going back to the car reference, they may have to remove a few brakes before they would be able to get in the mood. For example, the baby crying could be a brake that takes them out of the mood, or having recently argued with their partner could be a brake. For these individuals, each time a brake occurs, they need to start their desire/arousal process over again and work back into the mood with their partner.

In addition, desire itself can be very complex. Women and men change their desire levels across time. It is common right after a woman has a baby for her desire levels to plummet. Most people who have ever had a baby could understand why this occurs – you are so exhausted sex is often the last thing on your mind. Later in life, many men experience lower desire levels. They will state that it takes a little more effort to get an erection as they age. As clinicians, our job here is to normalize sexual desire differences and help couples identify ways their misunderstandings affect their sex life.

If you are interested in getting as much knowledge as possible on this subject, there are several books you can read to learn about the incredible complexity that is human sexual desire. *The Sex-starved Marriage* by Michele Weiner-Davis is one such helpful book for couples. Another good book is called *CPR for Your Sex Life: How to Breathe Life into a Dead, Dying or Dull Sex Life*, by Brown and Braveman. Another helpful book is Esther Perel's *Mating in Captivity*. Finally, I always encourage people to read Joannides's book, *The Guide to Getting It On*. For any further references, please visit the American Association of Sex Educators, Counselors, and Therapists website, AASECT.org, which is the certifying body for sex therapists in the United States.

A Good Story

For Noelle and Samuel, their sex life had gotten somewhat rough prior to Samuel's affair. Samuel met a woman at work. She and he exchanged numbers and started by texting each other. First, the texts seemed work related, but here and there the texts started to get flirtier, until it progressed to sexting. It was around this time that Noelle saw Samuel spending more time on his phone than with her. He also seemed less present day-to-day at home. Noelle found his texts and told him he had to break things off with the woman from work. Samuel immediately agreed to do so and felt very badly about the choice he made.

They came into therapy a few days after Noelle found the texts. She reported she was unsure if she could find a way to forgive him. I validated her worry and told her it was okay if she struggled to forgive for a while. Many of my clients do not forgive right away. It takes time. I suggested it could be helpful if she just came to therapy to talk about things and that it was okay for her to not make the choice initially.

Over the next few sessions, they worked on rebuilding trust and talking about various aspects of the relationship. At some point, Samuel brought up how their sex life seemed to falter after the first two years of the relationship. He stated that there could be many months that they would not be intimate. He had grown very dissatisfied in the relationship, but was still trying to be a good husband. Noelle agreed that their sex life did seem to change at that point. She also pointed out that she had suffered from some depression around that time in the relationship. It was hard for her to want sex when she felt so unhappy with life.

After exploring that time further, both partners had agreed that in many ways they had abandoned their relationship. The helpful part was that Samuel never excused his behavior for cheating. When cheating was discussed, he always took full responsibility for making his bad decision. He explained he should never have let things go that far and he felt deeply ashamed of himself. I think this helped Noelle to open up and have more conversations about the rest of the relationship. She knew their sex life had suffered but she didn't know what to do about things. The affair felt like a kick in the face.

As a part of their healing process, they both agreed to learn more about desire and sexuality. Noelle wanted to know that if Samuel ever felt abandoned again that he would talk to her about things and they would make a plan to fix things. Samuel agreed. He did not ever want to hurt her again and he knew he should have tried to talk to her. Many sessions were spent covering desire, what is normal and healthy, and how to address sexual problems when they occur. I reminded them that everyone goes through sexual problems. Instead of withdrawing from each other, they needed to find kind ways to bring up the issues and sometimes come back into therapy if this could be helpful to them.

After doing some work, they started an enjoyable sex life again. Along the way, they learned a few things too. Samuel did not know that the easiest way for a woman to orgasm during penetrative sex was if she was on top. He had avoided this position because he personally didn't like it as much, but as a result, Noelle was not experiencing orgasms during sex as frequently. Likewise, Noelle did not know that in order to get more frequent orgasms for herself, they needed to focus on clitoral stimulation. She thought that she should be able to orgasm with penis in vagina intercourse alone. Over time she had gotten tired of having sex that didn't include her own fulfillment. With a little guidance, they were able to become more flexible and generous lovers, which led to better sex and communication.

A Bad Story

Josh came into therapy individually because he believed he had a sex addiction. He had cheated multiple times on his wife and she had recently found out. She looked in his phone and found multiple numbers of prostitutes and women from Craigslist. He and she went to a separate couples counselor, but he came to me individually to work on his sex addiction.

The first part of therapy focused on assessment and diagnosis. As a sex therapist, I am bound by the ethical codes of my certifying body, AASECT. Officially, we do not use sex addiction to define problematic sexual behaviors. AASECT issued a position statement about this diagnosis that reads,

> AASECT 1) does not find sufficient empirical evidence to support the classification of sex addiction or porn addiction as a mental health disorder, and 2) does not find the sexual addiction training and treatment methods and educational pedagogies to be adequately informed by accurate human sexuality knowledge.
>
> (AASECT, 2016)

As a result of this position statement, sex therapists commonly start by adjusting the diagnosis for a client like this to something that fits but is also accepted by the DSM-V.

Clearly, in the case of this client, there were impulse control issues, sexually unethical practices, and repeated infidelities. While this client felt bad that his partner had found out about these indiscretions, it was also clear that he would have continued to seek these sexual experiences so long as his partner did not find out. I also tried to assess for sociopathic tendencies. There are clients who fall into a narcissistic personality disorder or antisocial personality disorder. He did not possess all of the requirements to meet either one of these diagnoses.

In a case like this, there are problematic sexual behaviors that have clearly affected this client's life and relationships. There is a book that AASECT accepts for the treatment of this behavior called *Treating Out of Control Sexual Behavior*, by Douglas Braun-Harvey and Michael Vigorito (2016). This book and treatment style attempts to approach out of control sexual behaviors from a research based treatment modality. As a part of treatment, I explained to the client that we do not advocate for a sex addiction diagnosis, but it is still very important for us to work as a team to help him start working on his ultimate goal of being faithful to his wife. He expressed feeling out of control when it came to his sexual urges.

One extra difficult challenge was that this client and his wife had lived in a sexless marriage at that point for five years. Now that she had found out he had been unfaithful, she did not want him to touch her at all. They had reached a standstill in their couples counseling. She was unwilling to move forward until she felt he was getting treatment for his sex addiction. Even then, she was unsure if she could ever forgive him.

He expressed some personal challenges with trying to be faithful in a sexless marriage. Long-term, he knew he could not be happy if they never had sex again. He discussed leaving her at some point if this were the case. I asked him different questions about what he valued in his marriage and what he struggled with. I explained that it would be good to give her time to see if she could forgive, especially if he valued the marriage. He was very impatient at times. One month into therapy, his wife still had not shown any affection towards him. At this point, he stated he thought he should leave. I explained to him that many people take years to heal from one infidelity, let alone multiple infidelities. This seemed to change his mind temporarily, but I could tell he was going to struggle with patience.

He asked how long he should give the marriage and how long he should wait to experience affection with his wife before he should end things. This was challenging for me because, on the one hand, I understand that sex is needed for a relationship to be fulfilling. On the other hand, his infidelities started before they had a sexless marriage. While a part of him justified his behavior by telling himself he was in a sexless marriage, there was still another part of him that acted this way even when they were having sex. Also, it is hard to put an exact date or time frame on when someone should give up on their relationship. The decision is a very personal one.

I told him it was okay for him to struggle in the relationship for a while. I suggested he talk to his wife about starting affection at some point. I also suggested he ask her what steps he could take to start building trust again so that one day they could be intimate again. If he needed to, I stated he could come up with an arbitrary deadline for how long he would give the relationship before moving on. He could keep this date in mind for himself (not to use as an ultimatum for her) so as not to get complacent. I suggested he put the date at about a year out. At that date, he could look at the relationship and see if there was some progress when it came to affection or if really they were not making any progress. I also suggested he should journal often about both his personal struggles and the small milestones he made with his wife. This way he would have some clear evidence from day-to-day activities to help him more objectively make the decision.

After four months of treatment, he and his wife still had not been affectionate. He decided to terminate treatment because he really just needed to let some time pass to see if things were going to change. He also felt he had some tools to help him control his sexual urges. He was avoiding pornography and keeping his phones and computer in the living room to hold himself accountable. He was going to continue journaling and working in couples counseling with his wife. Ultimately, his problems were not entirely fixed, but he was in a good enough spot to keep using his skills and to decide what choice to make when the year passed.

Your Human Self

This self-care section is very important to me as a sex therapist. I think that many people have this belief that if you do something for your job, you should be great at doing it in real life. This belief is very true in the case of a sex therapist. The general public, clinicians, and clients often assume that sex therapists should have a really great sex life. While we do know a lot about sex, our sex life is a work in progress like anything else in life. Just because you are helping your clients have a great sex life, doesn't mean you will have the perfect sex life every day.

I think that sex therapists can take it hard when their sex life is not as good as they would like it to be. We try very hard to learn the most up to date information about sexual health. We teach clients how to get more comfortable talking about sex. We usually tend to be a playful bunch because you have to develop a sense of humor when you say words like clitoris and ejaculation on a regular basis!

I am here to tell you all that it is completely normal for you to struggle in your sex life. There will be times where one or both of you suffers from sexual dysfunctions. There will be times when your own desire plummets and times when you struggle to see sex as fun or hot, not clinical. We are all human beings and we will suffer from many of the same sexual problems that our clients go through.

There are many things you can do to start back on a positive path with your partner. First, you can talk to each other. Sometimes, you just need to admit to your partner that you are unhappy with your sex life. That first step can then lead to other steps. Next, you can see your own therapist, read sexual health books together, or attend a conference on tantra or some other fun sexual topic.

One book I commonly refer to my clients is called *The Guide to Getting It On*, by Paul Joannides (2013). You and your partner can read a chapter at a time together and discuss the different topics in the book. One thing this book helps all couples do is laugh together about sex. It covers every topic about sex from A to Z and it really offers a fun perspective.

The one thing I think every clinician needs to be reminded of is that you are not a failure if you are struggling in your sex life. Also, your struggle does not mean you can't offer helpful sexual health guidance to your clients. Ultimately, we offer one thing to our clients that we can't offer in our relationships – objectivity. It's important to remember that this is why it can sometimes be easier to help a client than to help yourself. You are NOT as objective in your own life.

One additional thing you can do to help with your own sexual relationship is to start doing things alone with your partner again. Plan weekly date nights in which you try to be romantic with each other. You can go on outings that are active, like biking or snorkeling, or you can do dinner and a movie. One fun way to start feeling that connection again is to try new things with one another. Whether you go rock climbing for the first time or try a new wild restaurant where you don't get to use utensils, the newness of the activity can create a lasting memory that helps you bond. Either way, if you are struggling, do something about it. You deserve to be happy in your sex life too!

Note

* The full list of Good Enough Sex Principles is as follows:
1 Sex is a good element in life, an invaluable part of an individual's and couple's long-term comfort, confidence, intimacy, pleasure, and eroticism. Eroticism is an intentional feature and the responsibility of each partner.
2 Relationship and sexual satisfaction are the ultimate developmental focus and are essentially intertwined. The couple is an "intimate team" and together promote a vibrant balance of emotional intimacy and eroticism.
3 Accurate, realistic, age-appropriate, physiological, psychological, relationship, and sexual expectations are essential for sexual satisfaction.
4 Good physical health and healthy behavioral habits are vital for sexual health. Each individual values, respects, and affirms his/her partner's sexual body.
5 Relaxation is the foundation for pleasure and function.
6 Pleasure is as important as function.
7. Valuing variable, flexible sexual experiences and abandoning the "need" for perfect performance inoculates the couple against sexual dysfunction by reducing performance pressure, fears of failure, and rejection.
8 Five basic purposes for sex (pleasure, intimacy, stress reduction, self-esteem, reproduction) are integrated into the couple's sexual relationship. Sex for only one purpose, for extended periods of time, undermines flexibility and creates risk for sexual dysfunction and stress.
9 Integrate and flexibly use the three basic sexual arousal styles (sensual self-entrancement, partner interaction, and role enactment).
10 Partner gender differences and preferences are respectfully valued and similarities mutually accepted. Partners cooperate as an intimate team for relationship and sexual pleasure and satisfaction.
11 Sex is integrated into real life, and real life is integrated into sex. Partners ensure a "regular" frequency of sex. Sexuality is developing, growing, and evolving throughout one's life to create a unique sexual style. Regularity ensures an emotional "intimacy blender."
12 Sexuality is personalized; sex can be playful, spiritual, special.

(Metz & McCarthy, 2012)

Milestone 9 Forgiveness

Forgiveness is defined as the conscious choice to let go of resentment or vengeance towards an individual or group of people who caused harm to you (Greater Good, 2017), regardless of whether or not they deserve it. There are many reasons why forgiveness becomes a struggle in the situation of an affair. Does forgiveness mean that what my partner did was okay? If I forgive them, am I setting myself up to get hurt again? What if my partner doesn't deserve to be forgiven? Before your clients will be ready to forgive they will need to understand why forgiveness can be helpful.

Often, your clients will bring up the idea of forgiveness on their own. I would let your client bring this topic up first rather than pushing them to forgive before they are ready. Most of my clients struggling through infidelity have spent hours reading information online about the topic. In many of the online articles, forgiveness is discussed in some way or another. When clients broach the topic of forgiveness, I use motivational interviewing tactics to ask questions and allow them a space in therapy to explore forgiveness.

I ask questions such as, "Have you ever had something you needed to forgive someone for?" "Are you the kind of person who forgives easily or do you struggle to forgive?" "What process do you use to forgive someone?" This last question often will challenge my clients to really think about forgiveness in a more action oriented way. Many people have never really developed a process for forgiveness or did not know there was a way to intentionally forgive. This line of questioning can help clients explore the topic without feeling any sort of pressure to act (I will explain a process for forgiveness below in the intervention section).

Before suggesting your client should work on forgiving, it is good to help your client develop their own rationale for forgiveness. In an article written by the Mayo Clinic, they described several advantages to forgiveness, including: healthier relationships; greater spiritual and psychological well-being; less anxiety, stress, and hostility; lower blood pressure; fewer symptoms of depression; stronger immune system; improved heart health; higher self-esteem (Mayo Clinic Staff, 2017). In general, forgiveness focuses more on letting go of the hurt you feel as a result of an affair. The key for clients is to understand that forgiveness is done for their own emotional sanity. It does not mean that they have to accept their partner's behaviors as okay. Neither does it mean they have to put themselves at risk of future harm. In this next section, we will cover some helpful ways to address forgiveness.

Interventions

There are many articles that cover forgiveness. Often these can be religious in nature. As a clinician, I am deeply respectful of people's beliefs whether they are religious or not. In this section, I do not cover the religious aspects of forgiveness, because I want to offer universal tools of forgiveness. By all means, if a person has a religious leaning that can help them make this choice, encourage them to use that as their personal rationale for forgiveness. However, a person does not need to understand religion in order to benefit from the power of forgiving.

How to Teach Your Clients to Forgive

After working with several clients across the years, I have developed my own system of forgiveness. In various sessions, I have asked couples about their individual forgiveness process, and after listening to clients across the years, I have found some common themes. In this intervention, I cover the steps I feel are necessary to forgive someone. My own definition for how couples forgive includes the following steps:

1 Make an intentional choice to work towards forgiveness. Say to yourself, "I am going to forgive you over time."
2 Take time to empathize with your partner. Put yourself in their shoes. Try to develop an understanding of how it was possible for them to make a mistake of this magnitude. Do this over the course of the next several months. (This step is a hard one.)
3 When you are triggered or reminded of the hurt your partner caused, accept that you are still struggling with that hurt. Be kind to yourself and don't beat yourself up.
4 After accepting your struggle, intentionally shift your thoughts towards positive aspects in the relationship that are improving.
5 Remember that forgiveness is a process that takes time. Allow time to pass.

I have found that this explanation of forgiveness has helped many of my clients to rethink forgiving their partner.

Going back over the steps in detail, in Step 1, a client decides that they are willing to work towards forgiveness. They can state this out loud to their partner or they can start by discussing it with their clinician first until they are ready to discuss it with their partner. In their article about forgiveness in treatment, Fife et al. (2013) state that forgiveness is a decision characterized by the voluntary release of negative attitudes and feelings towards the offender. All that is happening in this step is an initial decision. It will take some time to get there, but the client chooses to work towards forgiveness. With that being said, it is easier to forgive a partner who is showing true remorse. It may take a while to get to forgiveness in some cases.

Stating it out loud is important because essentially the client is stating their intention. "I plan to do things over the course of the next few months to let go of this hurt." They may need to say this a few times to their partner. Often the unfaithful partner struggles with the thought that their partner will never get over what happened. If the unfaithful partner can be reminded that it is a process and it will take time, some of their anxiety can be calmed. You can coach the hurt partner to say things to the unfaithful partner like, "I am working towards forgiveness. I am not there yet, but the things you are doing to repair this are helping." When the unfaithful partner hears this, sometimes they are able to work on being patient. I try to coach the unfaithful partner to accept these comments as best as they can.

In Step 2, you can explain empathy in more detail. There is a big difference between asking open ended questions defensively versus using empathy. Asking open ended questions is one way that partners try to develop some empathy towards their partner. Questions such as, "What led you to spend more time alone with the other person?" or "How did you know things were getting out of control?" or "When did you know you were making a mistake?" can begin to help the hurt partner develop some understanding as to how their partner made the mistake. However, it can also lead to the hurt partner experiencing more emotional pain after discovering the information.

It is a tricky subject to cover. Empathy does help people to forgive, but how does one find a way to empathize with a person who lied to them and chose to be unfaithful? This is why it is incredibly important not to rush things with your clients. If you bring up forgiveness and meet resistance, they are not ready to forgive. One thing I bring up with clients is the capacity for all humans to harm others. In Fife et al.'s (2013) model of forgiveness, they suggest that individuals develop a view of their partner as imperfect and fallible, rather than innately bad or cruel. Essentially every person has the capability of causing hurt, and often they don't intend to cause hurt.

Eventually, as you lead the couples in working through some of the previous milestones, couples will start bringing up the topic of forgiveness. You will hear this in the way they speak to each other. They will talk with less defensiveness, choosing to listen to their partner with respect. This is the time when they are more able to develop empathy for some of their partner's choices. It is important to coach the unfaithful partner to decrease rationalization and blaming and take responsibility for their actions (Fife et al., 2013). The more this partner shows ownership and humility, the easier it is for the hurt partner to show empathy towards their mistake.

In Step 3, it is important to explain that forgiveness does not take all the pain away. Most couples are triggered with emotional hurt long after the infidelity. There are so many cultural references to infidelity, that it can often throw people off guard. Rather than viewing this hurt as a personal failing (i.e., I am a failure at forgiveness!), it is better to accept one's self. It's okay for forgiveness to take time. It's natural for memories of the pain to last for years afterwards. Accepting one's natural process allows it to happen. It is similar to showing empathy for yourself or forgiving yourself.

In Step 4, shifting thoughts towards the positive is helpful because it gives your clients something specific to do when they feel the hurt. It also builds resilience. You can coach them to ask themselves, "How has our relationship improved since then?" "What have I learned in this process about myself?" "How have we grown for the better?" "What am I thankful for?" These are conscious questions that guide clients towards resilience. Bad things happen to people all the time. While it was a hard time, in many ways an infidelity has a way of allowing couples to change their relationships for the better.

Finally in Step 5, forgiveness is a process. I often will restate this again and again so both partners remember it like a mantra. It takes time. When both partners deeply understand that forgiveness can take from months to years, they tend to be more forgiving of the process. I have had clients talk to me two years after an affair about their struggle to let go of the hurt. They feel as though something is wrong with them. It can be a huge help just to know that they are normal. There is nothing wrong with someone taking a large amount of time to forgive, because an infidelity is such a painful act to forgive. It's a betrayal that is very personal and feels like an attack on the marriage or long-term relationship. The worst part about it is that the attack came from within. Clients who use this process over time, report that they feel capable of forgiving but they will never forget.

Forgiveness When Clients Break Up

For Shelly and Jamie, they came to the conclusion that they no longer wished to be in a relationship anymore. Jamie had cheated on Shelly with several other women over the previous three years. The way Jamie explained it, she had checked out of the relationship long ago, but just never actually left or let Shelly know that she had moved on. Shelly found out about the affairs when she caught Jamie in their bed with another woman. After that, she scoured the phone records and found dozens of messages and meetings they shared.

At their first session, I found out they had been separated for over six months. Essentially this session was to help Shelly realize that Jamie was trying to end the relationship for good. She just didn't want to hurt Shelly by being that direct. I commonly offer an all-in-one session called the "Should I stay or should I go?" session. In it, couples spend three hours covering various topics in the relationship and trying to decide if it is worth salvaging. By the end of their session, it was made clear that Jamie was terminating the relationship for good. Shelly's new job was to come to terms with the break up.

Throughout this book, I have mostly been covering the stories of clients who decided to push through the aftermath of the affair and stay together. Each chapter has detailed several interventions focused on helping couples to work through any lingering issues. The reality is that some couples do break up. There are people who just cannot forgive their partners for what they did and need to move on. There are also partners like Shelly and Jamie, where the person who had the affair really was done with the relationship but needed that extra nudge to make their choice.

Regardless of how things end, there can be many leftover feelings that ex-partners struggle with while trying to get over the relationship. First, there is the typical grieving cycle that one goes through when one faces a serious loss. We covered the grief cycle in detail in Chapter 2. If someone does break up, I try to give a handout about the grief cycle to explain what they will go through as a result of losing the relationship.

Beyond the stages of grief, how do we help an individual forgive when the relationship ends? In a similar way to the process outlined above, I ask clients to consider reasons why it might be helpful for them to work towards forgiving their partner. I try not to rush this process because often the hurt partner is extremely hurt, grieving, and sometimes being uprooted from their life. Forgiveness should never be pressured on someone or rushed.

While they work through the grieving process, I often try to get the client thinking about what they want personally for their life. As angry as they might be towards their ex-partner, the reality is that the relationship is over. Dwelling on their partner can prevent them from making decisions to improve their own life.

Instead, I suggest they ask themselves what they need to be happy without their partner. Some individuals will struggle to answer this question so I offer the following guidance:

> I encourage you to remember back across the years you spent with your partner. Often when we have been married (in a relationship) for a long time, we say to ourselves, "I would love to do _____, but I can't because my partner would not want to do this." Think back to every time you said "no" to yourself. What were those things? Was it a cooking class? Did you want to start painting? Did you want to travel

to Italy? Whatever activity you wanted to do, start writing these down and identifying what you want for yourself alone. At some point, when you are ready, do them … just for you.

A long-term relationship requires a lot of compromise. If you add kids to the mix, there can be many excuses for why we can't spend our time in the way we would most prefer. "I'm too busy because I have to pick up the kids from their dance class," or "My husband and I only have a short amount of time to spend together. I want to spend it doing something we both enjoy." These thoughts are great ways to help a relationship work smoothly. Often, over the years we do sacrifice some of the things we personally love for the greater good of the relationship. I encourage my clients to make an effort over the next few months and even years to be intentional about doing things for themselves – to allow themselves to be selfish. I often find that this is one of the things that can help them begin to heal after losing their relationship.

After they really start to work on themselves, they tend to find it easier to work on forgiving their partner and letting go of the old hurt. One step that does change from the original steps of the forgiveness plan in the previous intervention is Step 4. In the intervention above, I suggested that the client remind themselves of the positive aspects of their current relationship. In the case of a relationship ending, Step 4 changes to the following: "After accepting your struggle, intentionally shift your thoughts towards positive aspects of your own life." Step 4 is still a part of the process, but it shifts for the newly single or divorced individual. In order for Step 4 to work, they have to have positive aspects in their new life without the other person. This is why it can be helpful to guide someone to focus on their own happiness after a divorce or break up. The more they work on themselves, the more they realize they need to let go of the leftover hurt.

Forgiveness with Consequences

Many clients believe that forgiveness leaves them exposed to future heart-ache. There is some truth to this. In order to let someone in, you open yourself up to both the potential good and the potential bad in that partner. You have to be vulnerable. You have to accept the possibility that they may cheat again and that you have no control over this. It seems safe to build up walls around your heart because it will protect you from potential hurt. The problem is that walls also protect you from experiencing the good in life. I am a firm believer that love is best expressed with every part of yourself, the good, the bad, and the ugly. I see this play out in many of the couples I watch work through this process. When they open up completely and show their brokenness, they become deeply intimate and connected in new ways, as they never have in the past. Both partners are forever changed.

For clients who are guarding their hearts with a barricade and can't decide to forgive, I introduce the concept of forgiveness with consequences. There is an old adage, "Forgive and forget." I explain to couples that no one will ever forget what happened during this betrayal. A client does not have to forget what happened, and, in some ways, can take steps to protect themselves from future hurts.

Essentially what I am suggesting is forgiving with real accountability set up for the future. This accountability can have many presentations. For one couple, the accountability is that partners will always have access to each other's emails and phones. In another couple, the accountability is a signed post-nuptial agreement in which financial consequences will result if an affair occurs again. In yet another couple, the hurt partner has a very clear plan set up for themselves for if an affair ever occurs again. This plan may include becoming more financially stable so they can leave if need be. Another plan may include places the person will go to separate, should another infidelity take place.

Whatever the plan, some clients need some sort of safety net to begin to move on and get comfortable in their relationship again. I do not judge or discourage the making of a plan. I think people need to feel some form of safety and they need the unfaithful partner to understand that this hurt cannot happen again. If there is a next time, there will be no therapy; no working out of problems; no third chances.

For clients who need this to move on, I give them examples of what other individuals have done to forgive with consequences. I help them develop their own tactical plan. I help them decide if they will tell the unfaithful partner about this plan, or if they will keep it to themselves. Either way, I respect their decision, and help them take any steps they feel are necessary to help them move on, should they personally want to do so.

A Realistic Story

Manny and Rachel were in therapy for two years. Manny was a pastor at a very big church. He was well known and well loved. Three years prior, Manny suffered from a terrible depression. He started to pull away from his wife, Rachel. She noticed he seemed off, but neither of them understood depression that well. They had also been taught through their religious background that depression was a type of spiritual weakness.

As the depression continued, Manny started behaving more erratically. He would get angry when his wife asked him to come home earlier or when she pointed out the longer hours he seemed to be working at the church. At some point, he was found in his office making love to his secretary. His co-pastor happened to walk into the office and found them. At that point, Manny had to make a big decision. The secretary was married and so was he.

Both Manny and his secretary admitted their affairs to their spouses. At that point, Manny and Rachel came into therapy. Manny felt terrible for how he had hurt his wife. He was deeply ashamed and embarrassed. Rachel was angry, hurt, and very embarrassed as well. How in the world could they come back from such a horrible event?

Over the next two years, they worked on their relationship in therapy. They explored Manny's depression in detail and developed a plan as a couple for addressing the depression proactively going forward. They also talked at length about all the details and the ways Rachel was hurt. They covered many of the milestones listed in this book.

At times, Rachel confessed to me that she did not know if she could ever fully forgive Manny for what he did. I did not push her towards it. I just gave her a space to explore this challenge and I even told her it was okay if she did not forgive him. They improved their relationship in different ways and in the second year did follow-up visits less frequently, until finally I stopped seeing them for a time.

A few years later, I called to see how things were going with them. I do this from time to time to check in on progress, or even to see if someone needs to come back in again. Rachel told me they were doing well. They still had bumps in the road. At times, an infidelity would show up in a show they were watching on TV or in a song they listened to. These reminders still hurt her. However, she had gotten better at feeling the pain for briefer periods and then refocusing on other things.

Manny continued to go above and beyond on special dates like their anniversary and birthdays. Rachel reported this really helped her feel like a priority to him. He would post big announcements on Facebook about how much she meant to him. On some of the harder days, it was helpful to see those messages and remember the love they shared.

While the incident happened long ago, she still was working towards forgiveness. Some days she did not even think about the incident. Other days, she was very sad. These days reminded her that while she had forgiven Manny, she could never forget it. Basically, she stated that forgiveness continued to be a work in progress. Over time, she hoped the infidelity would be a distant memory.

Your Human Self

For many therapists, a big portion of our work is focused on teaching couples and individuals how to work through problems, forgive or move on. Some people would say this is the very core of the therapeutic process. But what happens when we personally are struggling to forgive a person or situation that occurred to us?

I am a big fan of exploring counter-transference issues because as clinicians it is common for our day-to-day lives to present in our work. It may show up in a more intense reaction to a trauma story or an inability to validate a client's perspective. Whatever the case may be, I encourage you to continue to recognize areas where you experience counter-transference. It is likely that when this occurs, there is something you are still working out in your own life.

If there is someone or something you still need to forgive, I encourage you to explore this in your own life and take your own steps to work towards forgiveness. I am a firm believer in practicing what we preach. This means that if we are suggesting that a client works on forgiveness, then we should actively learn how to do this ourselves. Some of the best lessons I have ever learned in life came from practicing the very skills I suggest to my clients. Then I can actually speak to the challenge it may be to incorporate the skill in life.

A Hopeful Ending

Throughout this book, we have discussed various milestones that can help you guide your couples towards working through infidelity. I want to re-emphasize that each of these milestones takes time and energy. I do not expect couples to work through these milestones in any order, or even to achieve every milestone. There is no set time for how long it takes a couple to work through an infidelity. These chapters are simply meant to offer guidance for different ways you as the therapist can help.

The biggest challenge about infidelity is how it really hits people to the core. There is no easy way to come back when you feel your relationship is in shambles. I have come up with these specific milestones because I have seen that focusing on them has helped countless couples feel safer, knowing there is at least some path to recovery that they can take. There may be even more helpful steps that aren't included in this book.

The amazing thing to me about infidelity is how it can drive a couple to the brink while it can also motivate a couple to change their relationship for the better! I hope you can use this book to help your own couples rebuild their lives, with a deeper understanding of the realities regarding infidelity and a stronger relationship going forward.

References

AASECT. (November 29, 2016). AASECT Position Statement – Sex Addiction. (Given by email correspondence by Ian Kerner, PhD, LMFT.)

American Psychiatric Association. (2013). *Diagnostic and Statistical Manual of Mental Disorders* (5th Edition). Arlington, VA: American Psychiatric Publishing.

Atkins, D.C., Yi, J., Baucom, D.H., & Christensen, A. (2005). Infidelity in Couples Seeking Marital Therapy. *Journal of Family Psychology, 19*(3), 470–473. doi:10.1037/0893-3200.19.3.470.

Author Unknown. Benefit of the Doubt: Top Definition. (2016). Urban Dictionary Website. Online, available at: www.urbandictionary.com/define.php?term=Benefit%20of%20the%20doubt.

Author Unknown. Can Separated Couples Reconcile? (2016). Divorce Statistics Website. Online, available at: www.divorcestatistics.info/can-separated-couples-reconcile.html.

Author Unknown. Definition of Boundary. (2016). Merriam-Webster Dictionary Website. Online, available at: www.merriam-webster.com/dictionary/boundary.

Author Unknown. Definition of Forgiveness. (2017). Online, available at: http://greatergood.berkeley.edu/topic/forgiveness/definition.

Author Unknown. Definition of Privacy. (n.d.). *Collins English Dictionary – Complete and Unabridged* (10th Edition). Online, available at Dictionary.com Website: www.dictionary.com/browse/privacy. Accessed October 10, 2017.

Author Unknown. Personality Plays a Role in Infidelity. Truth about Deception. (2014). Online, available at: https://blog.truthaboutdeception.com/2014/08/25/personality-plays-a-role-in-infidelity/.

Author Unknown. What Is Forgiveness? (2017). *Greater Good* Website. Online, available at: https://greatergood.berkeley.edu/forgiveness/definition.

Author Unknown. Who Is Likely to Cheat. (2016). Online, available at: www.truthaboutdeception.com/cheating-and-infidelity/why-people-cheat/likely-to-cheat.html.

Baucom, D.H., Snyder, D.K., & Gordon, K.C. (2009). *Helping Couples Get Past the Affair: A Clinicians Guide*. New York: Guilford Press.

Berman, M.I. & Frazier, P.A. (2005). Relationship power and betrayal experience as predictors of reactions to infidelity. *Personality and Social Psychology Bulletin,* 31, 1617–1627.

Braun-Harvey, D., & Vigorito, M. (2016). *Treating Out of Control Sexual Behavior.* New York, NY: Springer Publishing Company.

Brown, M.L., & Braveman, S.L. (2007). *CPR for Your Sex Life: How to Breathe Life into a Dead, Dying or Dull Sex Life.* New York, NY: Booksurge.

Business Dictionary Website. (n.d.). Online, available at: www.businessdictionary. com/definition/accountability.html.

Butler, M.H. & Gardner, B.C. (2003). Adapting enactments to couples reactivity: five developmental stages. *Journal of Marital and Family Therapy*, 29, 311–327.

Cherry, K. (2016). What Is Resilience? (And Why It Matters). Online, available at: www.verywell.com/what-is-resilience-2795059.

DerSarkissian, C. (n.d.). What Are PTSD Triggers? Online, available at: www. webmd.com/mental-health/what-are-ptsd-triggers#2. Accessed June 30, 2017.

Diblasio, F.A. (2000). Decision-based Forgiveness Treatment in Cases of Marital Infidelity. *Psychotherapy: Theory, Research, Practice, Training, 37*(2), 149–158. doi:10.1037/h0087834.

Dietz, L. (2012). Validation. DBT Self Help Website. Online, available at: http:// dbtselfhelp.com/html/validation.html.

Dupree, W.J., White, M.B., Olson, C.S., & Lafluer, C.T. (2007). Infidelity Treatment Patterns: A Practice-based Evidence Approach. *The American Journal of Family Therapy*. doi:10.1080/01926180600969900.

Easton, D., & Hardy, J.W. (2009). *The Ethical Slut*. Berkeley, CA: Simon and Schuster.

Estroff Marano, H. (2012). From Promise to Promiscuity. *Psychology Today*. August, 63–69.

Fife, S.T., Weeks, G.R., & Stellberg-Filbert, J. (2013). Facilitating Forgiveness in the Treatment of Infidelity: An Interpersonal Model. *Journal of Family Therapy*, 35, 343–367. doi:10.1111/j.1467-6427.2011.00561.x.

Fruzzetti, A. (2006). *The High-conflict Couple: A Dialectical Behavior Therapy Guide to Finding Peace, Intimacy and Validation*. Oakland, CA: New Harbinger Publications.

Gottman, J.M., & Silver, N. (2015). *The Seven Principles for Making Marriage Work: A Practical Guide from the Country's Foremost Relationship Expert*. New York: Harmony Books.

Hartley, D. (2015). Meet the Machiavellians. Online, available at: www.psychology today.com/blog/machiavellians-gulling-the-rubes/201509/meet-the-machiavellians.

Jackman, M. (2014). Understanding the Cheating Heart: What Determines Infidelity Intentions? *Sexuality and Culture*. doi:10.1007/s12119-014-9248-z.

Joannides, P. (2013). *The Guide to Getting It On*. Saline, MI: Goofy Foot Press.

Khazan, O. (2014). Multiple Lovers without Jealousy. *The Atlantic*. Online, available at: www.theatlantic.com/health/archive/2014/07/multiple-lovers-no-jealousy/374697/.

Lally, P.M.V.J., Potts, H.W., & Wardle, J. (July 16, 2009). *How Are Habits Formed: Modelling Habit Formation in the Real World*. Online, available at: http://onlinelibrary.wiley.com/doi/10.1002/ejsp.674/abstract.

Leiblum, S.R. (2007). *Principles and Practice of Sex Therapy*. New York: The Guilford Press.

Linehan, M. (1993). *Skills Training Manual for Treating Borderline Personality Disorder*. New York, NY: The Guilford Press.

Linehan, M.M. (2014). *DBT Skills Training Handouts and Worksheets* (2nd Edition). New York, NY: The Guilford Press.

Luscombe, B. (2016). How to Stay Married. *TIME Magazine*. June Issue.

Maltz, W. (2012). Healing the Sexual Repercussions of Sexual Abuse. In Kleinplatz, P. (ed.), *New Directions in Sex Therapy: Innovations and Alternatives* (2nd Edition). New York, NY: Routledge, pp. 267–284.

Mayo Clinic Staff. (2017). Forgiveness: Letting Go of Grudges and Bitterness. Mayo Clinic Website. Online, available at: www.mayoclinic.org/healthy-lifestyle/adult-health/in-depth/forgiveness/art-20047692.

Metz, M.E., & McCarthy, B.W. (2007). The Good Enough Sex Model for Couple Satisfaction. *Sexual and Relationship Satisfaction, 22*(3), 351–361.

Metz, M.E. & McCarthy, B.W. (2012) The Good Enough Sex Model. In Kleinplatz, P. (ed.), *New Directions in Sex Therapy: Innovations and Alternatives* (2nd Edition). New York, NY: Routledge.

Mintz, L.B. (2017). *Becoming Cliterate: Why Orgasm Equality Matters – And How to Get It.* New York, NY: HarperOne, an imprint of HarperCollins.

Nagoski, E. (2015). *Come as You Are: The Surprising New Science that Will Transform your Sex Life.* Brunswick, Australia: Scribe Publications.

Nichols, M.P., & Schwartz, R.C. (2006). *Family Therapy: Concepts and Methods* (7th Edition). Boston: Pearson.

Norcross, J.C., Krebs, P.M., & Prochaska, J.O. (2011). Stages of Change. *Journal of Clinical Psychology, 67*(2), 143–152.

Oxford Dictionary: Intentions. (2017). Online, available at: https://en.oxford dictionaries.com/definition/intention.

Perel, E. (2007) *Mating in Captivity: Unlocking Erotic Intelligence.* New York, NY: Harper Paperbacks.

Rationalization (Psychology). (May 16, 2017). Online, available at: https://en. wikipedia.org/wiki/Rationalization_(psychology). Accessed May 19, 2017.

Rimmer, R.H. (1990). *The Harrad Experiment.* Amherst, NY: Prometheus Books.

Russell, V.M., & McNulty, J.K. (2013). Attachment Insecurity and Infidelity in Marriage. *Journal of Family Psychology, 27*(2). doi:10.1037/a0032118.

Schafer, M.H. (2014). Schema via Structure? Personal Network Density and the Moral Evaluation of Infidelity. *Sociological Forum, 29*(1). doi:10.1111/socf.12072.

Schneider, J.P., Weiss, R., & Samenow, C. (2012). Is It Really Cheating? Understanding the Emotional Reactions and Clinical Treatment of Spouses and Partners Affected by Cybersex Infidelity. *Sexual Addiction and Compulsivity, 19,* 123–139.

Sharpe, D.I., Walters, A.S., & Goren, M.J. (2005). Effect of Cheating Experience on Attitudes Toward Infidelity. *Sexuality and Culture, 17*(4), 643–658.

Snyder, D.K., Baucom, D.H., & Gordon, K.C. (2007). *Getting Past the Affair: A Program to Help You Cope, Heal, and Move On – Together or Apart.* New York: Guilford Press.

Solomon, S.D., & Teagno, L.J. (2006). *Intimacy after Infidelity: How to Rebuild and Affair-proof Your Marriage.* Oakland, CA: New Harbinger Publications.

Sprenkle, D., & Blow, A. (2004). Common Factors and Our Sacred Models. *Journal of Marital and Family Therapy, 30*(2), 113–129.

Spring, J.A. (2012). *After the Affair* (2nd Edition). New York, NY: William Morrow.

Tracy, N. (2016). Psychopathy: Definition, Symptoms, Signs and Causes – Psychopath – Personality Disorders. Online, available at: www.healthyplace.com/personality-disorders/psychopath/psychopathy-definition-symptoms-signs-and-causes/. Accessed May 19, 2017.

Urooj, A., Haque, A.U., & Anjum, G. (2015). Perception of Emotional and Sexual Infidelity among Married Men and Women. *Pakistan Journal of Psychological Research, 30*(2).

Weeks, G.R., Gambescia, N., & Jenkins, R.E. (2003). *Treating Infidelity: Therapeutic Dilemmas and Effective Strategies.* New York: W.W. Norton & Co.

Weiner-Davis, M. (1993). *Divorce Busting: A Step by Step Approach to Making Your Marriage Loving Again.* A Fireside Book.

Weiner-Davis, M. (2004). *The Sex-starved Marriage: Boosting Your Libido: A Couple's Guide.* New York, NY: Simon and Schuster.

Whisman, M.A., Gordon, K.C., & Chatav, Y. (2007). Predicting Sexual Infidelity in a Population-based Sample of Married Individuals. *Journal of Family Psychology, 21*(2), 320–324. doi:10.1037/0893-3200.21.2.320.

Index

accountability 46–47, 63, 69–70, 105
acknowledgment of pain caused 13–26;
  beginning of therapy 14–17; case
  studies 13, 21–25; grief cycle 17–18;
  interventions 17–21; letter of impact
  20–21, 22; meeting hurt partner's
  needs 16–17; ownership of the
  infidelity 15–16, 22; room for failure
  17; structured discussions 18–20
acting the opposite 23
action urges 1–2
affair proofing 45–47
affairs: definition of 2, 32, 37; ending it
  35–36; reasons for 27–31
After the Affair (Spring) 20, 70–71
assessment process 2–3

benefit of the doubt 63, 65
Berman, M.I. 32
borderline personality disorder 42
both/and approach 7, 33–34, 55–56
boundaries: in relationships 28–30,
  35–36; and trust 63–64, 66–67
Braun-Harvey, D. 79, 95

checking behavior 47
clarity 27–40; case studies 27, 28–29,
  30, 34–35, 36–39; contacting the
  'other' person 34–35; defining the
  affair 31–32; ending the affair 35–36;
  interventions 31–36; playing devil's
  advocate 32–34; timeline of treatment
  30–31; why people cheat 27–31
Come as You Are (Nagoski) 93
compulsive sexual behaviors 72, 95–97
confidentiality 24
conflict management 3–4
counter-transference issues 73, 81–82,
  106–107

DBT (dialectical behavior therapy) 1, 7,
  8, 9, 23, 33
depression 43, 105–106
desire 90, 92–93
devil's advocate 32–34
Diblasio, F.A. 14
DSM-V 42, 72
Dupree, W.J. 5, 18

earned trust 64
Easton, D. 78
emotion regulation 8
emotional affairs 13
empathy 14, 101–102
ending the affair 35–36
Estroff Marano, H. 17, 45–46, 53, 57,
  71
ethical dilemmas 11
Ethical Slut, The (Easton and Hardy)
  78

failure (of clients) 17
fidelity pact 70–71
Fife, S.T. 2, 4, 18, 39, 91, 101
forgiveness 13, 99–107; advantages of
  99–100; after break up 102–104;
  case studies 102–3, 105–106; with
  consequences 104–105; and empathy
  14, 101–102; interventions 100–105;
  self-care strategies 106–107; steps of
  100–102, 104; teaching 100–102
Frazier, P.A. 32
Fruzzetti, A. 8, 33

Good Enough Sex Model 87–88, 98
good relationship, characteristics of
  56–57
Gottman, J.M. 2, 56, 85
grief cycle 17–18

Guide to Getting it On, The
(Joannides) 97

Hardy, J.W. 78
Harrad Experiment, The (Rimmer) 78
High Conflict Couple, The (Fruzzetti) 8
honesty 67–68

impact of affair, reducing 1–12;
assessment process 2–3; case studies
6, 7, 9–11; discussions outside of
therapy 8; helpful interventions 5–8;
importance of task 1–2; role of
therapist 3–5
individualizing care 57–58
infidelity: definition of 2, 32, 37;
reasons for 27–31
intentions vs rationalizations 27–29

jealousy 68
Joannides, P. 97

Lally, P.M.V.J. 17
leaving or staying *see* staying or leaving
letter of impact 20–21, 22
Linehan, M. 89
love map 56–57
lying 39–40

Machiavellian personality 42
Maltz, W. 91
Mayo Clinic 99
McCarthy, B.W 88, 98
Metz, M.E. 88, 98
motivational interviewing 44, 99

Nagoski, E. 93
neutrality, maintaining 15
normalizing 77–78

online games 13
open relationships 75, 78–79

parenting skills 58
personality types prone to cheating 41–43
polyamory 75, 78–79
privacy 64, 69–70
psychopathy 42
PTSD symptoms 83–84, 91

rationalizations 27–30
redefining relationships 74–82; case
studies 77, 79–81; interventions
75–79; normalizing 77–78;

polyamory 75, 78–79; taking back
the relationship 75–76
reframes 65, 74
relationships, characteristics of good
ones 56–57
remorse 21
responsibility of therapists (for clients
choices) 40
responsive desire 90, 92–93
revenge affairs 6
Rimmer, R.H. 78
role of therapist 3–5

Schneider, J.P. 2, 83
Second Life (online game) 13
self-care strategies 11–12, 25–26,
39–40, 51–52, 60–61, 72–73, 81–82,
97–98, 106–107
separation 47–49
serenity prayer 40
*Seven Principles for Making Marriage
Work* (Gottman and Silver) 56
sex life 83–98; case studies 49–50,
87–88, 89, 90–92, 93–97; compulsive
sexual behaviors 72, 95–97; desires
and needs 90, 92–93; Good Enough
Sex Model 87–88; interventions
87–93; learning to talk about it 84–86;
no pressure system 89–90; polyamory
75, 78–79; role of therapist 86–87;
self-care strategies 97–98; trigger
response treatments 90–92
sexual desires and needs 90, 92–93
shielded enactments 18, 39
Silver, N. 2, 56, 85
softened startup 8
special dates 75–76, 80–81
spontaneous desire 92–93
Spring, J.A. 20, 70–71
staying or leaving 41–52; affair
proofing 45–47; case studies 46,
49–51; interventions 43–49;
personality types prone to cheating
41–43; self-care strategies 51–52;
separation 47–49
structured discussions 18–20
systems theory 55–56

teamwork 55–56
threats, eradicating 68–69
TIME Magazine 61
timeline, establishment of 5–6, 30–31
tracking behaviors 31
trauma response 83–84, 91

Treating Out of Control Sexual Behavior (Braun-Harvey and Vigorito) 95
trial separation 47–49
triggers 79–80, 84; trigger response treatments 90–92
trust, rebuilding 2, 10, 62–73; case studies 10, 62, 66, 67–68, 69, 70–72; eradicating threats 68–69; interventions 65–70; role of therapist 64–65; self-care strategies 72–73; and structured discussions 19–20; as two-way street 67–68; understanding trust 62–64

unresolved issues 53–61; case studies 53–54, 57, 58–60; individualizing care 57–58; interventions 55–58; teamwork 55–56; and traits of good relationship 56–57
Urooj, A. 15

validation 4, 7, 19, 22, 23–24, 56; levels of 8, 9
Vigorito, M. 79, 95
violence 6–7
vulnerabilities, identifying 45–46